CAMBRIDGE LIBRARY COLLECTION

Books of enduring scholarly value

Philosophy

This series contains both philosophical texts and critical essays about philosophy, concentrating especially on works originally published in the eighteenth and nineteenth centuries. It covers a broad range of topics including ethics, logic, metaphysics, aesthetics, utilitarianism, positivism, scientific method and political thought. It also includes biographies and accounts of the history of philosophy, as well as collections of papers by leading figures. In addition to this series, primary texts by ancient philosophers, and works with particular relevance to philosophy of science, politics or theology, may be found elsewhere in the Cambridge Library Collection.

Social Rights and Duties

Sir Leslie Stephen (1832–1904), the founding editor of the *Dictionary of National Biography*, and a writer on philosophy, ethics, and literature, was educated at Eton, King's College London and Trinity College, Cambridge, where he remained as a fellow and a tutor for a number of years. Though a sickly child, he later became a keen and successful mountaineer, taking part in first ascents of nine peaks in the Alps. In 1871 he became editor of the *Cornhill Magazine*. During his eleven-year tenure, he wrote two successful books on ethics, including *The Science of Ethics* in 1892, which was widely adopted as a standard textbook. This two-volume work, which was first published in 1896, brings together the lectures he gave to various ethical societies, mostly in London. In Volume 1, he considers the role of ethical societies and discusses a range of questions in politics, social equality and morality.

Cambridge University Press has long been a pioneer in the reissuing of out-of-print titles from its own backlist, producing digital reprints of books that are still sought after by scholars and students but could not be reprinted economically using traditional technology. The Cambridge Library Collection extends this activity to a wider range of books which are still of importance to researchers and professionals, either for the source material they contain, or as landmarks in the history of their academic discipline.

Drawing from the world-renowned collections in the Cambridge University Library, and guided by the advice of experts in each subject area, Cambridge University Press is using state-of-the-art scanning machines in its own Printing House to capture the content of each book selected for inclusion. The files are processed to give a consistently clear, crisp image, and the books finished to the high quality standard for which the Press is recognised around the world. The latest print-on-demand technology ensures that the books will remain available indefinitely, and that orders for single or multiple copies can quickly be supplied.

The Cambridge Library Collection will bring back to life books of enduring scholarly value (including out-of-copyright works originally issued by other publishers) across a wide range of disciplines in the humanities and social sciences and in science and technology.

Social Rights and Duties

Addresses to Ethical Societies

VOLUME 1

LESLIE STEPHEN

CAMBRIDGE
UNIVERSITY PRESS

CAMBRIDGE UNIVERSITY PRESS

Cambridge, New York, Melbourne, Madrid, Cape Town,
Singapore, São Paolo, Delhi, Tokyo, Mexico City

Published in the United States of America by Cambridge University Press, New York

www.cambridge.org
Information on this title: www.cambridge.org/9781108037020

© in this compilation Cambridge University Press 2011

This edition first published 1896
This digitally printed version 2011

ISBN 978-1-108-03702-0 Paperback

This book reproduces the text of the original edition. The content and language reflect
the beliefs, practices and terminology of their time, and have not been updated.

Cambridge University Press wishes to make clear that the book, unless originally published
by Cambridge, is not being republished by, in association or collaboration with, or
with the endorsement or approval of, the original publisher or its successors in title.

SOCIAL RIGHTS AND DUTIES

The Ethical Library

SOCIAL RIGHTS AND DUTIES

ADDRESSES TO ETHICAL SOCIETIES

BY

LESLIE STEPHEN

IN TWO VOLUMES

VOL. I.

LONDON

SWAN SONNENSCHEIN & CO., Limited

NEW YORK: MACMILLAN & CO.

1896

ABERDEEN UNIVERSITY PRESS.

NOTE.

THE following chapters are chiefly a republication of addresses delivered to the Ethical Societies of London. Some have previously appeared in the *International Journal of Ethics,* the *National Review,* and the *Contemporary Review.* The author has to thank the proprietors of these periodicals for their consent to the republication.

L. S.

CONTENTS.

	PAGE
THE AIMS OF ETHICAL SOCIETIES,	1
SCIENCE AND POLITICS,	45
THE SPHERE OF POLITICAL ECONOMY,	91
THE MORALITY OF COMPETITION,	133
SOCIAL EQUALITY,	175
ETHICS AND THE STRUGGLE FOR EXISTENCE,	221

THE AIMS OF ETHICAL SOCIETIES.*

I AM about to say a few words upon the aims of this society : and I should be sorry either to exaggerate or to depreciate our legitimate pretensions. It would be altogether impossible to speak too strongly of the importance of the great questions in which our membership of the society shows us to be interested. It would, I fear, be easy enough to make an over-estimate of the part which we can expect to play in their solution. I hold indeed, or I should not be here, that we may be of some service at any rate to each other. I think that anything which stimulates an active interest in the vital problems of the day deserves the support of all thinking men ; and I propose to consider briefly some of the principles by which we should be guided in doing whatever we can to promote such an interest.

We are told often enough that we are living in a period of important intellectual and social revolutions.

* Address to West London Ethical Society, 4th December, 1892.

In one way we are perhaps inclined even to state the fact a little too strongly. We suffer at times from the common illusion that the problems of to-day are entirely new : we fancy that nobody ever thought of them before, and that when we have solved them, nobody will ever need to look for another solution. To ardent reformers in all ages it seems as if the millennium must begin with their triumph, and that their triumph will be established by a single victory. And while some of us are thus sanguine, there are many who see in the struggles of to-day the approach of a deluge which is to sweep away all that once ennobled life. The believer in the old creeds, who fears that faith is decaying, and the supernatural life fading from the world, denounces the modern spirit as materialising and degrading. The conscience of mankind, he thinks, has become drugged and lethargic; our minds are fixed upon sensual pleasures, and our conduct regulated by a blind struggle for the maximum of luxurious enjoyment. The period in his eyes is a period of growing corruption; modern society suffers under a complication of mortal diseases, so widely spread and deeply seated that at present there is no hope of regeneration. The best hope is that its decay may provide the soil in which seed may be sown of a far-distant growth of happier augury. Such dismal forebodings are no novelty. Every age produces its prophecies of coming woes. Nothing would be easier than to make out a catena of testimonies from great men at every stage of the world's history, declaring each in turn that the cup of iniquity was now at last overflowing, and that corruption had reached so unprecedented a step that some great catastrophe must be approaching. A man of unusually lofty morality is, for that reason, more keenly sensitive to the lowness of the average standard, and too easily accepts the belief that the evils before his eyes must be in fact greater, and not, as may perhaps be the case, only more vividly perceived, than those of the bygone ages. A call to repentance easily takes the form of an assertion that the devil is getting the upper hand ; and we may hope that the pessimist view is only a form of the discontent which is a necessary condition of improvement. Anyhow, the diametrical conflict of prophecies suggests one remark which often impresses me. We are bound to call each other by terribly hard names. A gentleman assures me in print that I am playing the devil's game ; depriving my victims, if I have any, of all the beliefs that can make life noble or happy, and doing my best to destroy the very first principles of morality. Yet I meet my adversary in the flesh, and find that he

treats me not only with courtesy, but with no incon-
siderable amount of sympathy. He admits—by
his actions and his argument—that I—the miserable
sophist and seducer—have not only some good impulses, but have really something to say which
deserves a careful and respectful answer. An infidel,
a century or two ago, was supposed to have forfeited
all claim to the ordinary decencies of life. Now I
can say, and can say with real satisfaction, that I do
not find any difference of creed, however vast in
words, to be an obstacle to decent and even friendly
treatment. I am at times tempted to ask whether
my opponent can be quite logical in being so
courteous; whether, if he is as sure as he says that
I am in the devil's service, I ought not, as a matter
of duty, to be encountered with the old dogmatism
and arrogance. I shall, however, leave my friends
of a different way of thinking to settle that point for
themselves. I cannot doubt the sincerity of their
courtesy, and I will hope that it is somehow consistent with their logic. Rather I will try to meet
them in a corresponding spirit by a brief confession. I
have often enough spoken too harshly and vehemently
of my antagonists. I have tried to fix upon them too
unreservedly what seemed to me the logical consequences of their dogmas. I have condemned their
attempts at a milder interpretation of their creed as

proofs of insincerity, when I ought to have done more justice to the legitimate and lofty motives which prompted them. And I at least am bound by my own views to admit that even the antagonist from whose utterances I differ most widely may be an unconscious ally, supplementing rather than contradicting my theories, and in great part moved by aspirations which I ought to recognise even when allied with what I take to be defective reasoning. We are all amenable to one great influence. The vast shuttle of modern life is weaving together all races and creeds and classes. We are no longer shut up in separate compartments, where the mental horizon is limited by the area visible from the parish steeple; each little section can no longer fancy, in the old childish fashion, that its own arbitrary prejudices and dogmas are parts of the eternal order of things; or infer that in the indefinite region beyond, there live nothing but monsters and anthropophagi, and men whose heads grow beneath their shoulders. The annihilation of space has made us fellows as by a kind of mechanical compulsion; and every advance of knowledge has increased the impossibility of taking our little church—little in comparison with mankind, be it even as great as the Catholic Church—for the one pattern of right belief. The first effect of bringing remote nations and

classes into closer contact is often an explosion of
antipathy; but in the long run it means a development of human sympathy. Wide, therefore, as is
the opposition of opinions as to what is the true
theory of the world—as to which is the divine and
which the diabolical element—I fully believe that
beneath the war of words and dogmas there is a
growth of genuine toleration, and, we must hope, of
ultimate conciliation.

This is manifest in another direction. The
churches are rapidly making at least one discovery.
They are beginning to find out that their vitality
depends not upon success in theological controversy,
but upon their success in meeting certain social
needs and aspirations common to all classes. It is
simply impossible for any thinking man at the present
day to take any living interest, for example, in the
ancient controversies. The "drum ecclesiastic" of
the seventeenth century would sound a mere lullaby to
us. Here and there a priest or a belated dissenting
minister may amuse himself by threshing out once
more the old chaff of dead and buried dogmas.
There are people who can argue gravely about
baptismal regeneration or apostolical succession.
Such doctrines were once alive, no doubt, because
they represented the form in which certain still
living problems had then to present themselves.

They now require to be stated in a totally different shape, before we can even guess why they were once so exciting, or how men could have supposed their modes of attacking the question to be adequate. The Pope and General Booth still condemn each other's tenets; and in case of need would, I suppose, take down the old rusty weapons from the armoury. But each sees with equal clearness that the real stress of battle lies elsewhere. Each tries, after his own fashion, to give a better answer than the Socialists to the critical problems of to-day. We ought so far to congratulate both them and ourselves on the direction of their energies. Nay, can we not even co-operate, and put these hopeless controversies aside? Why not agree to differ about the questions which no one denies to be all but insoluble, and become allies in promoting morality? Enormous social forces find their natural channel through the churches; and if the beliefs inculcated by the church were not, as believers assert, the ultimate cause of progress, it is at least clear that they were not incompatible with progress. The church, we all now admit, whether by reason of or in spite of its dogmatic creed, was for ages one great organ of civilisation, and still exercises an incalculable in-fluence. Why, then, should we, who cannot believe in the dogmas, yet fall into line with believers for

practical purposes? Churches insist verbally upon
the importance of their dogma: they are bound to
do so by their logical position; but, in reality, for
them, as for us, the dogma has become in many
ways a mere excrescence—a survival of barren
formulæ which do little harm to anybody. Carlyle,
in his quaint phrase, talked about the exodus from
Houndsditch, but doubted whether it were yet time
to cast aside the Hebrew old clothes. They have
become threadbare and antiquated. That gives a
reason to the intelligent for abandoning them; but,
also, perhaps a reason for not quarrelling with those
who still care to masquerade in them. Orthodox
people have made a demand that the Board Schools
should teach certain ancient doctrines about the
nature of Christ; and the demand strikes some of us
as preposterous if not hypocritical. But putting aside
the audacity of asking unbelievers to pay for such
teaching, one might be tempted to ask, what harm
could it really do? Do you fancy for a moment that
you can really teach a child of ten the true meaning
of the Incarnation? Can you give him more than a
string of words as meaningless as magical formulæ?
I was brought up at the most orthodox of Anglican
seminaries. I learned the Catechism, and heard
lectures upon the Thirty-nine Articles. I never
found that the teaching had ever any particular effect

upon my mind. As I grew up, the obsolete exuviæ
of doctrine dropped off my mind like dead leaves
from a tree. They could not get any vital hold in
an atmosphere of tolerable enlightenment. Why
should we fear the attempt to instil these fragments
of decayed formulæ into the minds of children of
tender age? Might we not be certain that they
would vanish of themselves? They are superfluous,
no doubt, but too futile to be of any lasting importance. I remember that, when the first Education
Act was being discussed, mention was made of a
certain Jew who not only sent his son to a Christian
school, but insisted upon his attending all the
lessons. He had paid his fees, he said, for education in the Gospels among other things, and he
meant to have his money's worth. "But your son," it
was urged, "will become a Christian." "I," he replied,
"will take good care of that at home." Was not the
Jew a man of sense? Can we suppose that the
mechanical repetition of a few barren phrases will
do either harm or good? As the child develops he
will, we may hope, remember his multiplication table,
and forget his fragments of the Athanasian Creed.
Let the wheat and tares be planted together, and
trust to the superior vitality of the more valuable
plant. The sentiment might be expressed senti-
mentally as easily as cynically. We may urge, like

many sceptics of the last century, that Christianity should be kept "for the use of the poor," and renounced in the esoteric creed of the educated. Or we may urge the literary and æsthetic beauty of the old training, and wish it to be preserved to discipline the imagination, though we may reject its value as a historical statement of fact.

The audience which I am addressing has, I presume, made up its mind upon such views. They come too late. It might have been a good thing, had it been possible, to effect the transition from old to new without a violent convulsion: good, if Christian conceptions had been slowly developed into more simple forms; if the beautiful symbols had been retained till they could be impregnated with a new meaning; and if the new teaching of science and philosophy had gradually percolated into the ancient formulæ without causing a disruption. Possibly the Protestant Reformation was a misfortune, and Erasmus saw the truth more clearly than Luther. I cannot go into might-have-beens. We have to deal with facts. A conspiracy of silence is impossible about matters which have been vehemently discussed for centuries. We have to take sides; and we at least have agreed to take the side of the downright thinker, who will say nothing that he does not believe, and hide nothing that he does believe, and

speak out his mind without reservation or economy
and accommodation. Indeed, as things are, any
other course seems to me to be impossible. I have
spoken, for example, of General Booth. Many
people heartily admire his schemes of social reform,
and have been willing to subscribe for its support,
without troubling themselves about his theology.
I will make no objection; but I confess that I could
not therefore treat that theology as either morally or
intellectually respectable. It has happened to me
once or twice to listen to expositions from orators of
the Salvation Army. Some of them struck me as
sincere though limited, and others as the victims of
an overweening vanity. The oratory, so far as I
could hear, consisted in stringing together an endless
set of phrases about the blood of Christ, which, if they
really meant anything, meant a doctrine as low in the
intellectual scale as that of any of the objects of
missionary enterprise. The conception of the trans-
actions between God and man was apparently modelled
upon the dealings of a petty tradesman. The "blood
of Christ" was regarded like the panacea of a quack
doctor, which will cure the sins of anybody who
accepts the prescription. For anything I can say,
such a creed may be elevating—relatively: elevating
as slavery is said to have been elevating when
it was a substitute for extermination. The hymns of

the Army may be better than public-house melodies, and the excitement produced less mischievous than that due to gin. But the best that I can wish for its adherents is, that they should speedily reach a point at which they could perceive their doctrines to be debasing. I hope, indeed, that they do not realise their own meaning: but I could almost as soon join in some old pagan ceremonies, gash my body with knives, or swing myself from a hook, as indulge in this variety of spiritual intoxication.

There are, it is true, plenty of more refined and intellectual preachers, whose sentiments deserve at least the respect due to tender and humane feeling. They have found a solution, satisfactory to themselves, of the great dilemma which presses on so many minds. A religion really to affect the vulgar must be a superstition; to satisfy the thoughtful, it must be a philosophy. Is it possible to contrive so to fuse the crude with the refined as to make at least a working compromise? To me personally, and to most of us living at the present day, the enterprise appears to be impracticable. My own experience is, I imagine, a very common one. When I ceased to accept the teaching of my youth, it was not so much a process of giving up beliefs, as of discovering that I had never really believed. The contrast between the genuine convictions which guide and govern our conduct, and the professions which we were taught to repeat in church, when once realised, was too glaring. One belonged to the world of realities, and the other to the world of dreams. The orthodox formulæ represent, no doubt, a sentiment, an attempt to symbolise emotions which might be beautiful, or to indicate vague impressions about the tendency of things in general; but to put them side by side with real beliefs about facts was to reveal their flimsiness. The "I believe" of the creed seemed to mean something quite different from the "I believe" of politics and history and science. Later experience has only deepened and strengthened that feeling. Kind and loving and noble-minded people have sought to press upon me the consolations of their religion. I thank them in all sincerity; and I feel,—why should I not admit it?— that it may be a genuine comfort to set your melancholy to the old strain in which so many generations have embodied their sorrows and their aspirations. And yet to me, its consolation is an invitation to reject plain facts; to seek for refuge in a shadowy world of dreams and conjectures, which dissolve as you try to grasp them. The doctrine offered for my acceptance cannot be stated without qualifications and reserves and modifications, which make it as useless as it is vague and conjectural. I may learn in time to submit to the inevitable; I cannot drug myself with phrases which evaporate as soon as they are exposed to a serious test. You profess to give me the only motives of conduct; and I know that at the first demand to define them honestly—to say precisely what you believe and why you believe it— you will be forced to withdraw, and explain and evade, and at last retire to the safe refuge of a mystery, which might as well be admitted at starting. As I have read and thought, I have been more and more impressed with the obvious explanation of these observations. How should the beliefs be otherwise than shadowy and illusory, when their very substance is made of doubts laboriously and ingeniously twisted into the semblance of convictions? In one way or other that is the characteristic mark of the theological systems of the present day. Proof is abandoned for persuasion. The orthodox believer professed once to prove the facts which he asserted and to show that his dogmas expressed the truth. He now only tries to show that the alleged facts don't matter, and that the dogmas are meaningless. Nearly two centuries ago, for example, a deist pointed out that the writer of the Book of Daniel, like other people, must have written after the events which he mentioned. All the learned, down to Dr. Pusey, denounced his theory, and declared his argument to be utterly destructive of the faith. Now an orthodox professor will admit that the deist was perfectly right, and only tries to persuade himself that arguments from facts are superfluous. The supposed foundation is gone: the superstructure is not to be affected. What the keenest disputant now seeks to show is, not that the truth of the records can be established beyond reasonable doubt; but that no absolute contradiction in terms is involved in supposing that they correspond more or less roughly to something which may possibly have happened. So long as a thing is not proved false by mathematical demonstration, I may still continue to take it for a divine revelation, and to listen respectfully when experienced statesmen and learned professors assure me with perfect gravity that they can believe in Noah's flood or in the swine of Gadara. They have an unquestionable right to believe if they please: and they expect me to accept the facts for the sake of the doctrine. There, unluckily, I have a similar difficulty. It is the orthodox who are the systematic sceptics. The most famous philosophers of my youth endeavoured to upset the deist by laying the foundation of Agnosticism, arbitrarily tagged to an orthodox conclusion. They told me to believe a doctrine because it was totally impossible that I should know whether it was true or not, or indeed attach any

real meaning to it whatever. The highest altar, as
Sir W. Hamilton said, was the altar to the unknown
and unknowable God. Others, seeing the inevitable
tendency of such methods, have done their best to
find in that the Christian doctrine, rightly understood,
the embodiment of the highest philosophy. It is the
divine voice which speaks in our hearts, though
it has caught some accretion of human passion
and superstition. The popular versions are false and
debased ; the old versions of the Atonement, for
example, monstrous ; and the belief in the everlasting
torture of sinners, a hideous and groundless carica-
ture. With much that such men have said I could,
of course, agree heartily; for, indeed, it expresses the
strongest feelings which have caused religious revolt.
But would it not be simpler to say, " the doctrine is
not true," than to say, " it is true, but means just the
reverse of what it was also taken to mean " ? I prefer
plain terms; and " without doubt he shall perish
everlastingly " seems to be an awkward way of
denying the endlessness of punishment. You cannot
denounce the immorality of the old dogmas with the
infidel, and then proclaim their infinite value with
the believer. You defend the doctrine by showing
that in its plain downright sense,—the sense in which
it embodied popular imaginations,—it was false and
shocking. The proposal to hold by the words

evacuated of the old meaning is a concession of the whole case to the unbeliever, and a substitution of sentiment and aspiration for a genuine intellectual belief. Explaining away, however dexterously and delicately, is not defending, but at once confessing error, and encumbering yourself with all the trammels of misleading associations. The more popular method, therefore, at the present day is not to rationalise, but to try to outsceptic the sceptic. We are told that we have no solid ground from reason at all, and that even physical science is as full of contradictions as theology. Such enterprises, con-ducted with whatever ingenuity, are, as I believe, hopeless; but at least they are fundamentally and radically sceptical. That, under whatever disguises, is the true meaning of the Catholic argument, which is so persuasive to many. To prove the truth of Christianity by abstract reasoning may be hopeless; but nothing is easier than to persuade yourself to believe it, if once you will trust instinct in place of reason, and forget that instinct proves anything and everything. The success of such arguments with thoughtful men is simply a measure of the spread of scepticism. The conviction that truth is unattain-able is the master argument for submitting to "authority". The "authority," in the scientific sense of any set of men who agree upon a doctrine,

VOL. I.

varies directly as their independence of each other. Their "authority" in the legal sense varies as the closeness of their mutual dependence. As the consent loses its value logically, it gains in power of coercion. And therefore it is easy to substitute drilling for arguing, and to take up a belief as you accept admission to a society, as a matter of taste and feeling, with which abstract logic has nothing to do. The common dilemma—you must be a Catholic or an atheist—means, that theology is only tenable if you drill people into belief by a vast organisation appealing to other than logical motives.

I do not argue these points: I only indicate what I take to be your own conviction as well as mine. It seems to me, in fact, that the present state of mind —if we look to men's real thoughts and actions, not to their conventional phrases—is easily definable. It is simply a tacit recognition that the old orthodoxy cannot be maintained either by the evidence of facts or by philosophical argument. It has puzzled me sometimes to understand why the churches should insist upon nailing themselves down to the truth of their dogmas and their legendary history. Why cannot they say frankly, what they seem to be constantly on the verge of saying—Our dogmas and our history are not true, or not "true" in the

historical or scientific sense of the word? To ask
for such truth in the sphere of theology is as
pedantic as to ask for it in the sphere of poetry.
Poetical truth means, not that certain events actually
happened, or that the poetical " machinery " is to be
taken as an existing fact; but that the poem is, so
to speak, the projection of truths upon the cloudland
of imagination. It reflects and gives sensuous
images of truth; but it is only the Philistine or
the blockhead who can seriously ask, is it true?
Some such position seems to be really conceivable
as an ultimate compromise. Put aside the prosaic
insistence upon literal matter-of-fact truth, and we
may all agree to use the same symbolism, and
interpret it as we please. This seems to me
to be actually the view of many thoughtful
people, though for obvious reasons it is not
often explicitly stated. One reason is, of course,
the consciousness that the great mass of mankind
requires plain, tangible motives for governing its
life ; and if it once be admitted that so much of the
orthodox doctrine is mere symbolism or adumbration
of truths, the admission would involve the loss of the
truths so indicated. Moral conduct, again, and
moral beliefs are supposed to depend upon some
affirmation of these truths; and excellent people are
naturally shy of any open admission which may

appear to throw doubt upon the ultimate grounds of
morality.

Indeed, if it could be really proved that men have
to choose between renouncing moral truths and accepting unproved theories, it might be right—I will
not argue the point—to commit intellectual suicide.
If the truth is that we are mere animals or mere
automata, shall we sacrifice the truth, or sacrifice
what we have at least agreed to call our higher
nature? For us the dilemma has no force: for we do
not admit the discrepancy. We believe that morality
depends upon something deeper and more permanent
than any of the dogmas that have hitherto been
current in the churches. It is a product of human
nature, not of any of these transcendental speculations or faint survivals of traditional superstitions.
Morality has grown up independently of, and often
in spite of, theology. The creeds have been good
so far as they have accepted or reflected the moral
convictions; but it is an illusion to suppose that
they have generated it. They represent the dialect
and the imagery by which moral truths have been
conveyed to minds at certain stages of thought; but
it is a complete inversion of the truth to suppose
that the morality sprang out of them. From this
point of view we must of necessity treat the great
ethical questions independently. We cannot form

a real alliance with thinkers radically opposed to us. Divines tell us that we reject the one possible basis of morality. To us it appears that we are strengthening it, by severing it from a connection with doctrines arbitrary, incapable of proof, and incapable of retaining any consistent meaning Theologians once believed that hell-fire was the ultimate sentence, and persecution the absolute duty of every Christian ruler. The churches which once burnt and exterminated are now only anxious to proclaim freedom of belief, and to cast the blame of persecution upon their rivals. Divines have discovered that the doctrine of hell-fire deserves all that infidels have said of it; and a member of Dante's church was arguing the other day that hell might on the whole be a rather pleasant place of residence. Doctrines which can thus be turned inside out are hardly desirable bases for morality. So the early Christians, again, were the Socialists of their age, and took a view of Dives and Lazarus which would commend itself to the Nihilists of to-day. The church is now often held up to us as the great barrier against Socialism, and the one refuge against subversive doctrines. In a well-known essay on "People whom one would have wished to have seen," Lamb and his friends are represented as agreeing that if Christ were to enter they would all

fall down and worship Him. It may have been so ;
but if the man who best represents the ideas of early
Christians were to enter a respectable society of to-
day, would it not be more likely to send for the
police ? When we consider such changes, and mark
in another direction how the dogmas which once set
half the world to cut the throats of the other half,
have sunk into mere combinations of hard words, can
we seriously look to the maintenance of dogmas,
even in the teeth of reason, as a guarantee for ethical
convictions ? What you call retaining the only base
of morality, appears to us to be trying to associate
morality with dogmas essentially arbitrary and
unreasonable.

From this point of view it is naturally our opinion
that we should promote all thorough discussion of
great ethical problems in a spirit and by methods
which are independent of the orthodox dogmas.
There are many such problems undoubtedly of the
highest importance. The root of all the great social
questions of which I have spoken lies in the region
of Ethics ; and upon that point, at least, we can go
along with much that is said upon the orthodox side.
We cannot, indeed, agree that Ethics can be ade-
quately treated by men pledged to ancient traditions,
employing antiquated methods, and always tempted
to have an eye to the interest of their own creeds

and churches. But we can fully agree that ethical
principles underlie all the most important problems.
Every great religious reform has been stimulated
by the conviction that the one essential thing is a
change of spirit, not a mere modification of the
external law, which has ceased to correspond to
genuine beliefs and powerful motives. The commonest criticism, indeed, of all projectors of new
Utopias is that they propose a change of human
nature. The criticism really suggests a sound
criterion. Unless the change proposed be practicable, the Utopia will doubtless be impossible. And
unless some practicable change be proposed, the
Utopia, even were it embodied in practice, would be
useless. If the sole result of raising wages were an
increase in the consumption of gin, wages might as
well stay at a minimum. But the tacit assumption
that all changes of human nature are impracticable
is simply a cynical and unproved assertion. All of
us here hold, I imagine, that human nature has in a
sense been changed. We hold that, with all its
drawbacks, progress is not an illusion; that men
have become at least more tolerant and more
humane ; that ancient brutalities have become impossible ; and that the suffering of the weaker excites
a keener sympathy. To say that, in that sense,
human nature must be changed, is to say only that

the one sound criterion of all schemes for social
improvement lies in their ethical tendency.   The
standard of life cannot be permanently raised unless
you can raise the standard of motive.   Old-fashioned
political theorists thought that a simple change of
the constitutional machinery would of itself remedy
all evils, and failed to recognise that behind the
institutions lie all the instincts and capabilities of the
men who are to work them.   A similar fallacy is
prevalent, I fancy, in regard to what we call social
reforms.   Some scheme for a new mode of distributing the products of industry would, it is often
assumed, remedy all social evils.   To my thinking,
no such change would do more than touch the superficial evils, unless it had also some tendency to call
out the higher and repress the lower impulses.
Unless we can to some extent change " human
nature," we shall be weaving ropes of sand, or
devising schemes for perpetual motion, for driving
our machinery more effectively without applying
fresh energy.   We shall be falling into the old
blunders; approving Jack Cade's proposal—as re-
corded by Shakespeare—that the three-hooped pot
should have seven hoops ; or attempting to get rid
of poverty by converting the whole nation into
paupers.   No one, perhaps, will deny this in terms;
and to admit it frankly is to admit that every scheme

must be judged by its tendency to " raise the manhood of the poor," and to make every man, rich and
poor, feel that he is discharging a useful function in
society. Old Robert Owen, when he began his
reforms, rested his doctrine and his hopes of per-
fectibility upon the scientific application of a scheme
for " the formation of character ".   His plans were
crude enough, and fell short of success. But he had
seen the real conditions of success; and when, in
after years, he imagined that a new society might be
made by simply collecting men of any character in a
crowd, and inviting them to share alike, he fell into
the inevitable failure. Modern Socialists might do
well to remember his history.

Now it is, as I understand, primarily the aim of
an Ethical Society to promote the rational discussion
of these underlying ethical principles. We wish to
contribute to the clearest understanding we can of
the right ends to which human energy should be
devoted, and of the conditions under which such
devotion is most likely to be rewarded with success.
We desire to see the great controversy carried on in
the nearest possible approach to a scientific spirit.
That phrase implies, as I have said, that we must
abandon much of the old guidance. The lights by
which our ancestors professed to direct their course
are not for us supernatural signs, shining in a

transcendental region, but at most the beacons which they had themselves erected, and valuable as indications, though certainly not as infallible guides, to the right path. We must question everything, and be prepared to modify or abandon whatever is untenable. We must be scientific in spirit, in so far as we must trust nothing but a thorough and systematic investigation of facts, however the facts may be interpreted. Undoubtedly, the course marked out is long and arduous. It is perfectly true, moreover, as our antagonists will hasten to observe, that professedly scientific reasoners are hardly better agreed than their opponents. If they join upon some negative conclusions, and upon some general principles of method, they certainly do not reach the same results. They have at present no definite creed to lay down. I need only refer, for example, to one very obvious illustration. The men who were most conspicuous for their attempt to solve social problems by scientific methods, and most confident that they had succeeded, were, probably, those who founded the so-called " classical " political economy, and represented what is now called the individualist point of view. Government, they were apt to think, should do nothing but stand aside, see fair-play, and keep our knives from each other's throats and our hands out of each other's pockets,

Much as their doctrines were denounced, this view is still represented by the most popular philosopher of the day. And undoubtedly we shall do well to take to heart the obvious moral. If we still believe in the old-fashioned doctrines, we must infer that to work out a scientific doctrine is by no means to secure its acceptance. If we reject them we must argue that the mere claim to be scientific may inspire men with a premature self-confidence, which tends only to make their errors more systematic. When, however, I look at the actual course of controversy, I am more impressed by another fact. " Individualism " is sometimes met by genuine argument. More frequently, I think, it is met by simple appeal to sentiment. This kind of thing, we are told, is exploded ; it is not up to date; it is as obsolete as the plesiosaurus; and therefore, without bothering ourselves about your reasoning, we shall simply neglect it. Talk as much as you please, we can get a majority on the other side. We shall disregard your arguments, and, therefore—it is a common piece of logic at the present day—your arguments must be all wrong. I must be content here with simply indicating my own view. I think, in fact, that, in this as in other cases, the true answer to extreme theorists would be very different. I hold that we would begin by admitting the immense value of the lesson taught by the old individualists, if that be their right name. If they were precipitate in laying down "iron laws" and proclaiming inexorable necessity, they were perfectly right in pointing out that there are certain "laws of human nature," and conditions of social welfare, which will not be altered by simply declaring them to be unpleasant. They did an inestimable service in emphatically protesting against the system of forcibly suppressing, or trying to suppress, deep-seated evils, without an accurate preliminary diagnosis of the causes. And—not to go into remote questions—the "individualist" creed had this merit, which is related to our especial aims. The ethical doctrine which they preached may have had—I think that it had—many grave defects; but at least it involved a recognition of the truth which their opponents are too apt to shun or reject. They, at least, asserted strenuously the cardinal doctrine of the importance of individual responsibility. They might draw some erroneous inferences, but they could not put too emphatically the doctrine that men must not be taught to shift the blame of all their sufferings upon some mysterious entity called society, or expect improvement unless, among other virtues, they will cultivate the virtue of strenuous, unremitting, masculine self-help.

If this be at all true, it may indicate what I take to

be the aim of our society, or rather of us as members of an ethical society. We hold, that is, that the great problems of to-day have their root, so to speak, in an ethical soil. They will be decided one way or other by the view which we take of ethical questions. The questions, for example, of what is meant by social justice, what is the justification of private property, or the limits of personal liberty, all lead us ultimately to ethical foundations. The same is, of course, true of many other problems. The demand for political rights of women is discussed, rightly no doubt, upon grounds of justice, and takes us to some knotty points. Does justice imply the equality of the sexes; and, if so, in what sense of " equality " ? And, beyond this, we come to the question, What would be the bearing of our principles upon the institution of marriage, and upon the family bond ? No question can be more important, or more vitally connected with Ethics. We, at any rate, can no longer answer such problems by any traditional dogmatism. They—and many other questions which I need not specify—have been asked, and have yet to be answered. They will probably not be answered by a simple yes or no, nor by any isolated solution of a metaphysical puzzle. Undoubtedly, a vast mass of people will insist upon being consulted, and will adopt methods which cannot be regarded as philosophical. Therefore, it is a matter of pressing importance that all people who can think at all should use their own minds, and should do their best to widen and strengthen the influence of the ablest thinkers. The chaotic condition of the average mind is our reason for trying to strengthen the influence, always too feeble, of the genuine thinkers. Much that passes itself off for thought is simply old prejudice in a new dress. Tradition has always this, indeed, to say for itself: that it represents the product of much unconscious reasoning from experience, and that it is at least compatible with such progress as has been hitherto achieved. Progress has in future to take place in the daylight, and under the stress of keen discussion from every possible point of view. It would be rash indeed to assume that we can hope to see the substitution of purely rational and scientific methods for the old haphazard and tentative blundering into slightly better things. It is possible enough that the creed of the future may, after all, be a compromise, admitting some elements of higher truth, but attracting the popular mind by concessions to superstition and ignorance. We can hardly hope to get rid of the rooted errors which have so astonishing a vitality. But we should desire, and, so far as in us lies, endeavour to secure the presence of the largest possible element of genuine and reasoned conviction in the faith of our own and the rising generation.

I have not sought to say anything new. I have only endeavoured to define the general position which we, as I imagine, have agreed to accept. We hold in common that the old dogmas are no longer tenable, though we are very far from being agreed as to what should replace them. We have each, I dare say, our own theory; we agree that our theories, whatever they may be, are in need of strict examination, of verification, it may be, but it may be also of modification or rejection. We hope that such societies as this may in the first place serve as centres for encouraging and popularising the full and free discussion of the great questions. We wish that people who have reached a certain stage of cultivation should be made aware of the course which is being taken by those who may rightly claim to be in the van. We often wish to know, as well as we can, what is the direction of the deeper currents of thought; what genuine results, for example, have been obtained by historical criticism, especially as applied to the religious history of the world; we want to know what are the real points now at issue in the world of science; the true bearing of the theories of evolution, and so forth, which are known by name far beyond the circle in which their logical reasoning is really appreciated ; we want to know, again, what are the problems which really interest modern metaphysicians or psychologists; in what directions there seems to be a real promise of future achievement, and in what directions it seems to be proved by experience that any further expansion of intellectual energy is certain to result only in the discovery of mares' nests.

Matthew Arnold would have expressed this by saying that we are required to be made accessible to the influence of the Zeitgeist. There is a difficulty, no doubt, in discovering by what signs we may recognise the utterances of the Zeitgeist ; and distinguish between loyalty to the real intellectual leaders and a simple desire to be arrayed in the last new fashion in philosophy. There is no infallible sign ; and, yet, a genuine desire to discover the true lines in which thought is developing, is not of the less importance. Arnold, like others, pointed the moral by a contrast between England and Germany. The best that has been done in England, it is said, has generally been done by amateurs and outsiders. They have, perhaps, certain advantages, as being less afraid to strike into original paths, and even the originality of ignorance is not always, though it may be in nine cases out of ten, a name for fresh blundering. But if sporadic English writers have

now and then hit off valuable thoughts, there can be
no doubt that we have had a heavy price to pay.
The comparative absence of any class, devoted, like
German professors, to a systematic and combined
attempt to spread the borders of knowledge and
speculation, has been an evil which is the more felt
in proportion as specialisation of science and famili-
arity with previous achievements become more important.   It would be very easy to give particular
instances of our backwardness.   How different
would have been the course of English church
history, said somebody, if Newman had only known
German!   He would have breathed a larger air, and
might have desisted—I suppose that was the meaning
—from the attempt to put life into certain dead
bones.   And with equal truth, it may be urged, how
much better work might have been done by J. S.
Mill if he had really read Kant!   He might not have
been converted, but he would have been saved from
maintaining in their crude form, doctrines which undoubtedly require modification.   Under his reign,
English thought was constantly busied with false
issues, simply from ignorance of the most effective
criticism.   It is needless to point out how much time
is wasted in the defence of positions that have long
been turned by the enemy from sheer want of
acquaintance with the relevant evidence, or with

the logic that has been revealed by the slow thrashing out of thorough controversy. It would be invidious perhaps to insist too much upon another obvious result : the ease with which a man endowed with a gift of popular rhetoric, and a facility for catching at the current phrases, can set up as a teacher, however palpable to the initiated may be his ignorance. Scientific thought has perhaps as much to fear from the false prophets who take its name as from the open enemies who try to stifle its voice. I would rather emphasise another point, perhaps less generally remarked. The study has its idols as well as its market-place. Certain weaknesses are developed in the academical atmosphere as well as in the arenas of public discussion. Freeman used to say that English historians had avoided certain errors into which German writers of far greater knowledge and more thorough scholarship had fallen, simply because points were missed by a professor in a German university which were plain to those who, like many Englishmen, had to take a part in actual political work. I think that this is not without a meaning for us. We have learnt, very properly, to respect German research and industry ; and we are trying in various directions to imitate their example. Perhaps it would be as well to keep an eye upon some German weaknesses. A philosophy made by

professors is apt to be a philosophy for pedants. A
professor is bound to be omniscient ; he has to have
an answer to everything ; he is tempted to construct
systems which will pass muster in the lecture-room,
and to despise the rest of their applicability to daily
life. I confess myself to be old-fashioned enough
to share some of the old English prejudices against
those gigantic structures which have been thrown out
by imposing philosophers, who evolved complete
systems of metaphysics and logic and religion and
politics and æsthetics out of their own consciousness.
We have multiplied professors of late, and professors
are bound to write books, and to magnify the value
of their own studies. They must make a show of
possessing an encyclopædic theory which will explain
everything and take into account all previous theories.
Sometimes, perhaps, they will lose themselves in
endless subtleties and logomachies and construct
cobwebs of the brain, predestined to the rubbish-
heap of extinct philosophies. It is enough, however,
to urge that a mere student may be the better for
keeping in mind the necessity of keeping in mind
real immediate human interests ; as the sentimental-
ist has to be reminded of the importance of strictly
logical considerations. And I think too that a
very brief study of the most famous systems of old
days will convince us that philosophers should be

content with a more modest attitude than they have
sometimes adopted; give up the pretensions to
framing off-hand theories of things in general, and be
content to puzzle out a few imperfect truths which
may slowly work their way into the general structure
of thought. I wish to speak humbly as befits one
who cannot claim any particular authority for his
opinion. But, in all humility, I suggest that if we
can persuade men of reputation in the regions where
subtle thought and accurate research are duly valued,
we shall be doing good, not only to ourselves, but, if
I may whisper it, to them. We value their attain-
ments so highly that we desire their influence to
spread beyond the narrow precinct of university
lecture-rooms; and their thoughts be, at the same
time, stimulated and vitalised by bringing them into
closer contact with the problems which are daily
forced upon us in the business of daily life. A
divorce between the men of thought and the men of
action is really bad for both. Whatever tends to
break up the intellectual stupor of large classes, to
rouse their minds, to increase their knowledge of the
genuine work that is being done, to provide them
even with more of such recreations as refine and
invigorate, must have our sympathy, and will be
useful both to those who confer and to those who
receive instruction. So, after all, a philosopher can

learn few things of more importance than the art of translating his doctrines into language intelligible and really instructive to the outside world. There was a period when real thinkers, as Locke and Berkeley and Butler and Hume, tried to express themselves as pithily and pointedly as possible. They were, say some of their critics, very shallow: they were over-anxious to suit the taste of wits and the town: and in too much fear of the charge of pedantry. Well, if some of our profounder thinkers would try for once to pack all that they really have to say as closely as they can, instead of trying to play every conceivable change upon every thought that occurs to them, I fancy that they would be surprised both at the narrowness of the space which they would occupy and the comparative greatness of the effect they would produce.

An ethical society should aim at supplying a meeting-place between the expert and specialist on one side, and, on the other, with the men who have to apply ideas to the complex concretes of political and social activity. How far we can succeed in furthering that aim I need not attempt to say. But I will conclude by reverting to some thoughts at which I hinted at starting. You may think that I have hardly spoken in a very sanguine or optimistic tone. I have certainly admitted the existence of enormous difficulties and the probabilities of very imperfect success. I cannot think that the promised land of which we are taking a Pisgah sight is so near or the view so satisfactory as might be wished. A mirage like that which attended our predecessors may still be exercising illusions for us ; and I anticipate less an immediate fruition, than a beginning of another long cycle of wanderings through a desert, let us hope rather more fertile than that which we have passed. If this be something of a confession you may easily explain it by personal considerations. In an old controversy which I was reading the other day, one of the disputants observed that his adversary held that the world was going from bad to worse. "I do not wonder at the opinion," he remarks; "for I am every day more tempted to embrace it myself, since every day I am leaving youth further behind." I am old enough to feel the force of that remark. Without admitting senility, I have lived long enough, that is, to know well that for me the brighter happiness is a thing of the past ; that I have to look back even to realise what it means ; and to feel that a sadder colouring is conferred upon the internal world by the eye "which hath kept watch o'er man's mortality". I have watched the brilliant promise of many contemporaries eclipsed by premature death ; and have too often had to apply Newton's remark,

" If that man had lived, we might have known something ". Lights which once cheered me have gone
out, and are going out all too rapidly; and, to
say nothing of individuals, I have also lived long
enough to watch the decay of once flourishing beliefs.
I can remember, only too vividly, the confident hope
with which many young men, whom I regarded as
the destined leaders of progress, affirmed that the
doctrines which they advocated were going forth con-
quering and to conquer; and though I may still
think that those doctrines had a permanent value,
and were far from deserving the reproaches now often
levelled at them, I must admit that we greatly exaggerated our omniscience. I am often tempted, I confess, to draw the rather melancholy moral that some of
my younger friends may be destined to disillusionment,
and may be driven some thirty years hence to admit
that their present confidence was a little in excess.

I admit all this : but I do not admit that my view
could sanction despondency. I can see perhaps
ground for foreboding which I should once have
rejected. I can realise more distinctly, not only the
amount of misery in the world, but the amount of
misdirected energy, the dulness of the average
intellect, and the vast deadweight of superstition and
dread of the light with which all improvement must
have to reckon. And yet I also feel that, if a com-

placent optimism be impossible, the world was never so full of interest. When we complain of the stress and strain and over-excitement of modern society we indicate, I think, a real evil; but we also tacitly admit that no one has any excuse for being dull. In every direction there is abundant opportunity for brave and thoughtful men to find the fullest occupation for whatever energy they may possess. There is work to be found everywhere in this sense, and none but the most torpid can find an excuse for joining the spiritually unemployed. The fields, surely, are white for the harvest, though there are weeds enough to be extirpated, and hard enough furrows to be ploughed. We know what has been done in the field of physical science. It has made the world infinite. The days of the old pagan, "suckled in some creed outworn," are regretted in Wordsworth's sonnet; for the old pagan held to the poetical view that a star was the chariot of a deity. The poor deity, however, had, in fact, a duty as monotonous as that of a driver in the Underground Railway. To us a star is a signal of a new world; it suggests universe beyond universe; sinking into the infinite abysses of space; we see worlds forming or decaying and raising at every moment problems of a strange fascination. The prosaic truth is really more poetical than the old figment of the childish

imagination. The first great discovery of the real
nature of the stars did, in fact, logically or not,
break up more effectually than perhaps any other
cause, the old narrow and stifling conception of the
universe represented by Dante's superlative power;
and made incredible the systems based on the conception that man can be the centre of all things and the
universe created for the sake of this place. It is
enough to point to the similar change due to modern
theories of evolution. The impassable barriers of
thought are broken down. Instead of the verbal
explanation, which made every plant and animal an
ultimate and inexplicable fact, we now see in each
a movement in an indefinite series of complex
processes, stretching back further than the eye can
reach into the indefinite past. If we are sometimes
stunned by the sense of inconceivable vastness, we
feel, at least, that no intellectual conqueror need
ever be affected by the old fear. For him there will
always be fresh regions to conquer. Every discovery
suggests new problems; and though knowledge may
be simplified and codified, it will always supply a
base for fresh explanations of the indefinite regions
beyond. Can that which is true of the physical
sciences be applied in any degree to the so-called
moral sciences? To Bentham, I believe, is ascribed
the wish that he could fall asleep and be waked at

the end of successive centuries, to take note of the
victories achieved in the intervals by his utilitarianism.
Tennyson, in one of his youthful poems, played with
the same thought.   It would be pleasant, as the
story of the sleeping beauty suggested, to rise every
hundred years to mark the progress made in science
and politics; and to see the " Titanic forces " that
would come to the birth in divers climes and seasons;
for we, he says—

> For we are Ancients of the earth,
> And in the morning of the times.

Tennyson, if this expressed his serious belief,
seems to have lost his illusions; and it is probable
enough that Bentham's would have had some unpleasant surprises could his wish have been granted.
It is more than a century since his doctrine was first
revealed, and yet the world has not become converted;
and some people doubt whether it ever will be.   If,
indeed, Bentham's speculations had been adopted; if
we had all become convinced that morality means
aiming at the greatest happiness of the greatest
number; if we were agreed as to what is happiness,
and what is the best way of promoting it,—there would
still have been a vast step to take, no less than to
persuade people to desire to follow the lines of conduct which tend to minimise unhappiness.   The
mere intellectual conviction that this or that will be
useful is quite a different thing from the desire.

You no more teach men to be moral by giving them
a sound ethical theory, than you teach them to be
good shots by explaining the theory of projectiles. A
religion implies a philosophy, but a philosophy is not
by itself a religion.   The demand that it should be
is, I hold, founded upon a wrong view as to the relation
between the abstract theory and the art of conduct.
To convert the world you have not merely to prove
your theories, but to stimulate the imagination, to
discipline the passions, to provide modes of utterance
for the emotions and symbols which may represent
the fundamental beliefs—briefly, to do what is done
by the founders of the great religions.   To transmute
speculation into action is a problem of tremendous
difficulty, and I only glance in the briefest way at
its nature.   We, I take it, as members of Ethical
Societies, have no claim to be, even in the humblest
way, missionaries of a new religion : but are simply
interested in doing what we can to discuss in a
profitable way the truths which it ought to embody
or reflect.   But that is itself a work of no trifling
importance ; and we may imagine that a Bentham,
refreshed by his century's slumber, and having
dropped some of his little personal vanities, would
on the whole be satisfied with what he saw.   If
Bacon could again come to life, he too would find
that the methods which he contemplated and the

doctrines which he preached were narrow and re-
futive; yet his prophecies of scientific growth have
been more than realised by his successors, modifying,
in some ways, rejecting his principles. And so
Bentham might hold to-day that, although his sacred
formula was not so exhaustive or precise as he fancied,
yet the conscious and deliberate pursuit of the happiness of mankind had taken a much more important
place in the aspirations of the time. He would see
that the vast changes which have taken place in
society, vast beyond all previous conception, were
bringing up ever new problems, requiring more
elaborate methods, and more systematic reasoning.
He would observe that many of the abuses which
he denounced have disappeared, and that though
progress does not take place along the precise lines
which he laid down, there is both a clearer recognition of the great ends of conduct, and a general
advance in the direction which he desired. That
this can be carried on by promoting a free and full
discussion of first principles; that the great social
evils which still exist can be diminished, and the
creed of the future, however dim its outlines may
be to our perception, may be purified as much as
possible from ancient prejudice and superstition, is
our faith; and however little we can do to help in
carrying out that process, we desire to do that little.

SCIENCE AND POLITICS.*

IT is with great pleasure that I address you as president of this Society. Your main purpose, as I understand, is to promote the serious study of political and social problems in a spirit purged from the prejudice and narrowness of mere party conflict. You desire, that is, to promote a scientific investigation of some of the most important topics to which the human mind can devote itself. There is no purpose of which I approve more cordially: yet the very statement suggests a doubt. To speak of science and politics together is almost to suggest irony. And if politics be taken in the ordinary sense; if we think of the discussions by which the immediate fate of measures and of ministries is decided, I should be inclined to think that they belong to a sphere of thought to which scientific thought is hardly applicable, and in which I should be personally an unwarrantable intruder. My friends have sometimes accused me, indeed, of indifference

* Address to the Social and Political Education League, 29th March, 1892.

to politics. I confess that I have never been able
to follow the details of party warfare with the interest
which they excite in some minds: and reasons,
needless to indicate, have caused me to stray
further and further away from intercourse with the
society in which such details excite a predominant—
I do not mean to insinuate an excessive—interest. I
feel that if I were to suggest any arguments bearing
directly upon home rule or disestablishment, I should
at once come under that damnatory epithet "academical," which so neatly cuts the ground from
under the feet of the political amateur. Moreover,
I recognise a good deal of justice in the implied
criticism. An active politician who wishes to im-
press his doctrines upon his countrymen, should
have a kind of knowledge to which I can make no
pretension. I share the ordinary feelings of awful
reverence with which the human bookworm looks
up to the man of business. He has faculties which
in me are rudimentary, but which I can appreciate
by their contrast to my own feebleness. The
"knowledge of the world" ascribed to lawyers, to
politicians, financiers, and such persons, like the
"knowledge of the human heart" so often ascribed
to dramatists and novelists, represents, I take it, a
very real kind of knowledge; but it is rather an instinct than a set of definite principles; a power of

somehow estimating the tendencies and motives of their fellow-creatures in a mass by rule of thumb, rather than by any distinctly assignable logical process; only to be gained by long experience and shrewd observation of men and cities. Such a faculty, as it reaches sound results without employing explicit definitions and syllogisms and inductive processes, sometimes inclines its possessors to look down too contemptuously upon the closet student.

While, however, I frankly confess my hopeless incapacity for taking any part in the process by which party platforms are constructed, I should be ashamed to admit that I was not very keenly interested in political discussions which seem to me to touch vitally important matters. And fully recognising the vast superiority of the practical man in his own world, I also hold that he should not treat me and my like as if we, according to the famous comparison, were black beetles, and he at the opposite pole of the universe. There exists, in books at least, such a thing as political theory, apart from that claiming to underlie the immediate special applications. Your practical man is given to appealing to such theories now and then; though I confess that he too often leaves the impression of having taken them up on the spur of the moment to round a peroration and to give dignity to a popular cry:

and that, in his lips, they are apt to sound so crude
and artificial that one can only wonder at his con-
descending to notice them. He ridicules them as
the poorest of platitudes whenever they are used
by an antagonist, and one can only hope that his
occasional homage implies that he too has a certain
belief that there ought to be, and perhaps may
somewhere be, a sound theory, though he has not
paid it much attention. Well, we, I take it, differ
from him simply in this respect, that we believe
more decidedly that such theory has at least a
potential existence; and that if hitherto it is a very
uncertain and ambiguous guide, the mere attempt to
work it out seriously may do something to strengthen
and deepen our practical political convictions. A
man of real ability, who is actively engaged in
politics without being submerged by merely political
intrigues, can hardly fail to wish at least to institute
some kind of research into the principles which guide
his practice. To such a desire we may attribute
some very stimulating books, such, for example, as
Bagehot's *Physics and Politics* or Mr. Bryce's philosophical study of the United States. What I propose
to do is to suggest a few considerations as to the
real value and proper direction of these arguments,
which lie, as it were, on the borderland between
the immediate " platform " and the abstract theory.

Philosophers have given us the name "Sociology"—a barbarous name, say some—for the science
which deals with the subject matter of our inquiries.
Is it more than a name for a science which may or
may not some day come into existence? What is
science? It is simply organised knowledge; that
part of our knowledge which is definite, established
beyond reasonable doubt, and which achieves its
task by formulating what are called "scientific
laws". Laws in this sense are general formulæ,
which, when the necessary data are supplied, will
enable us to extend our knowledge beyond the immediate facts of perception. Given a planet, moving
at a given speed in a given direction, and controlled
by given attractive forces, we can determine its place
at a future moment. Or given a vegetable organism
in a given environment, we can predict within certain
limits the way in which it will grow, although the
laws are too obscure and too vague to enable us to
speak of it with any approach to the precision of
astronomy. And we should have reached a similar
stage in sociology if from a given social or political
constitution adopted by a given population, we could
prophesy what would be the results. I need not say
that any approximation to such achievements is
almost indefinitely distant. Personal claims to such
powers of prediction rather tend to bring discredit

upon the embryo science.   Coleridge gives in the
Biographia Literaria a quaint statement of his own
method.   On every great occurrence, he says, he
tried to discover in past history the event that
most nearly resembled it.   He examined the
original authorities.   " Then fairly subtracting the
points of difference from the points of likeness," as
the balance favoured the former or the latter, he
conjectured that the result would be the same, or
different.   So, for example, he was able to prophesy
the end of the Spanish rising against Napoleon from
the event of the war between Philip II. and the Dutch
provinces.   That is, he cried, " Heads ! " and on
this occasion the coin did not come down tails.   But
I need hardly point out how impossible is the
process of political arithmetic.   What is meant by
adding or subtracting in this connection ?   Such a
rule of three would certainly puzzle me, and, I
fancy, most other observers.   We may say that the
insurrection of a patriotic people, when they are
helped from without, and their oppressors have to
operate from a distant base and to fight all Europe
at the same time, will often succeed ; and we may
often be right ; but we should not give ourselves the
airs of prophets on that account.   There are many
superficial analogies of the same character.   My
predecessor, Professor Dicey, pointed out some of

them, to confirm his rather depressing theory that
history is nothing but an old almanac. Let me
take a common one, which, I think, may illustrate
our problem. There is a certain analogy between
the cases of Cæsar, Cromwell, and Napoleon. In
each case we have a military dictatorship as the
final outcome of a civil war. Some people imagined
that this analogy would apply to the United States,
and that Washington or Grant would be what was
called the man on horseback. The reasoning really
involved was, in fact, a very simple one. The
destruction of an old system of government makes
some form of dictatorship the only alternative to
chaos. It therefore gives a chance to the one indisputable holder of power in its most unmistakable
shape, namely, to the general of a disciplined army.
A soldier accordingly assumed power in each of the
three first cases, although the differences between the
societies ruled by the Roman, the English and the
French dictators are so vast that further comparison
soon becomes idle. Neither Washington nor Grant
had the least chance of making themselves dictators
had they wished, because the civil wars had left governments perfectly uninjured and capable of discharging
all their functions, and had not produced a regular
army with interests of its own. In this and other
cases, I should say that such an analogy may be

to some extent instructive, but I should certainly
deny that there was anything like a scientific induc-
tion. We, happily, can reason to some extent upon
political matters by the help of simple common
sense before it has undergone that process of
organisation, of reduction to precise measurable
statements, which entitles it to be called a scientific
procedure. The resemblance of Washington to Cromwell was of the external and superficial order. It
may be compared to those analogies which exist
between members of different natural orders without implying any deeper resemblance. A whale,
we know, is like a fish in so far as he swims
about in the sea, and he has whatever fishlike
qualities are implied in the ability to swim.
He will die on land, though not from the
same causes. But, physiologically, he belongs
to a different race, and we should make blunders if
we argued from the external likeness to a closer resemblance. Or, to drop what may be too fanciful a
comparison, it may be observed that all assemblies
of human beings may be contrasted in respect of
being numerous or select, and have certain properties in consequence. We may therefore make some
true and general propositions about the contrasts between the action of small and large consultative bodies
which will apply to many widely different cases. A

good many, and, I think, some really valuable observations of this kind have been made, and form the substance of many generalisations laid down as to the relative advantages of democracy and aristocracy. Now I should be disposed to say that such remarks belong rather to the morphology than the physiology of the social organism. They indicate external resemblances between bodies of which the intimate constitution and the whole mode of growth and conditions of vitality, may be entirely different. Such analogies, then, though not without their value, are far from being properly scientific.

What remains? There is, shall we say, no science of sociology—merely a heap of vague, empirical observations, too flimsy to be useful in strict logical inference? I should, I confess, be apt to say so myself. Then, you may proceed, is it not idle to attempt to introduce a scientific method? And to that I should emphatically reply, No! it is of the highest importance. The question, then, will follow, how I can maintain these two positions at once. And to that I make, in the first place, this general answer: Sociology is still of necessity a very vague body of approximate truths. We have not the data necessary for obtaining anything like precise laws. A mathematician can tell you precisely what

he means when he speaks of bodies moving under
the influence of an attraction which varies inversely
as the square of the distance.   But what are the
attractive forces which hold together the body
politic? They are a number of human passions,
which even the acutest psychologists are as yet quite
unable to analyse or to classify: they act according
to laws of which we have hardly the vaguest inkling;
and, even if we possessed any definite laws, the facts
to which they have to be applied are so amazingly
complex as to defy any attempt at assigning results.
There is, so far as I can see, no ground for supposing
that there is or ever can be a body of precise truths
at all capable of comparison with the exact sciences.
But this obvious truth, though it implies very narrow
limits to our hopes of scientific results, does not force
us to renounce the application of scientific method.
The difficulty applies in some degree even to physiology as compared with physics, as the vital
phenomena are incomparably more complex than
those with which we have to deal in the simpler
sciences; and yet nobody doubts that a scientific
physiology is a possibility, and, to some extent, a
reality.   Now, in sociology, however imperfect it
may be, we may still apply the same methods which
have been so fruitful in other departments of thought.
We may undertake it in the scientific spirit which

depends upon patient appeal to observation, and be guided by the constant recollection that we are dealing with an organism, the various relations of whose constituent parts are determined by certain laws to which we may, perhaps, make some approximation. We may do so, although their mutual actions and reactions are so complex and subtle that we can never hope to disentangle them with any approach to completeness. And one test of the legitimacy of our methods will be, that although we do not hope to reach any precise and definitely assignable law, we yet reach, or aim at reaching, results which, while wanting in precision, want precision alone to be capable of incorporation in an ideal science such as might actually exist for a supernatural observer of incomparably superior powers. A man who knows, though he knows nothing more, that the moon is kept in its orbit by forces similar to or identical with those which cause the fall of an apple, knows something which only requires more definite treatment to be made into a genuine theory of gravitation. If, on the contrary, he merely pays himself with words, with vague guesses about occult properties, or a supposed angel who directs the moon's course, he is still in the unscientific stage. His theory is not science still in the vague, but something which stops the way to science. Now, if

we can never hope to get further than the step which
in the problem of gravitation represents the first step
towards science, yet that step may be a highly important one. It represents a diversion of the current
of thought from such channels as end in mere shifting sands of speculation, into the channel which leads
towards some definite conclusion, verifiable by experience, and leading to conclusions, not very precise,
but yet often pointing to important practical results.
It may, perhaps, be said that, as the change which I
am supposing represents only a change of method
and spirit, it can achieve no great results in actual
assignable truth.   Well! a change of method and
spirit is, in my opinion, of considerable importance,
and very vague results would still imply an improvement in the chaos of what now passes for political
philosophy.   I will try to indicate very briefly the
kind of improvement of which we need not despair.

First of all, I conceive that, as I have indicated,
a really scientific habit of thought would dispel many
hopeless logomachies. When Burke, incomparably
the greatest of our philosophical politicians, was
arguing against the American policy of the Government, he expressed his hatred of metaphysics—the
" Serbonian bog," as he called it, in which whole
armies had been lost.   The point at which he aimed
was the fruitless discussion of abstract rights, which

prevented people from applying their minds to the actual facts, and from seeing that metaphysical entities of that kind were utterly worthless when they ceased to correspond to the wants and aspirations of the peoples concerned. He could not, as he said, draw up an indictment against a nation, because he could not see how such troubles as had arisen between England and the Colonies were to be decided by technical distinctions such as passed current at *nisi prius*. I am afraid that the mode of reasoning condemned by Burke has not yet gone out of fashion. I do not wish to draw down upon myself the wrath of metaphysicians. I am perfectly willing that they should go on amusing themselves by attempting to deduce the first principles of morality from abstract considerations of logical affirmation and denial. But I will say this, that, in any case, and whatever the ultimate meaning of right and wrong, all political and social questions must be discussed with a continual reference to experience, to the contents as well as to the form of their metaphysical concepts. It is, to my mind, quite as idle to attempt to determine the value, say, of a political theory by reasoning independent of the character and circumstances of the nation and its constituent members, as to solve a medical question by abstract formulæ, instead of by careful, prolonged, and searching investigation into the constitution of the human body. I think that this requires to be asserted so long as popular orators continue to declaim, for example, about the "rights of man," or the doctrines of political equality. I by no means deny, or rather I should on due occasion emphatically assert, that the demands covered by such formulæ are perfectly right, and that they rest upon a base of justice. But I am forced to think that, as they are generally stated, they can lead to nothing but logomachy. When a man lays down some such sweeping principle, his real object is to save himself the trouble of thinking. So long as the first principles from which he starts are equally applicable,—and it is of the very nature of these principles that they should be equally applicable to men in all times and ages, to Englishmen and Americans, Hindoos and Chinese, Negroes and Australians,—they are worthless for any particular case, although, of course, they may be accidentally true in particular cases. In short, leaving to the metaphysicians—that is, postponing till the Greek Kalends—any decision as to the ultimate principles, I say that every political theory should be prepared to justify itself by an accurate observation of the history and all the various characteristics of the social organisation to which it is to be applied.

This points to the contrast to which I have referred:

the contrast between the keen vigorous good sense
upon immediate questions of the day, to which I
often listen with the unfeigned admiration due to the
shrewd man of business, and the paltry little outworn
platitudes which he introduces when he wants to tag
his arguments with sounding principles. I think, to
take an example out of harm's way, that an excellent
instance is found in the famous American treatise,
the *Federalist*. It deserves all the credit it has won
so long as the authors are discussing the right way
to form a constitution which may satisfy the wants
and appease the prejudices then actually existing.
In spite of such miscalculations as beset all forecasts
of the future, they show admirable good sense and
clear appreciation. But when they think it necessary
to appeal to Montesquieu, to tag their arguments
from common sense with little ornamental formulæ
learnt from philosophical writings, they show a very
amiable simplicity; but they also seem to me to sink
at once to the level of a clever prize essay in a university competition. The mischief may be slight
when we are merely considering literary effect. But
it points to a graver evil. In political discussions,
the half-trained mind has strong convictions about
some particular case, and then finds it easiest to
justify its conviction by some sweeping general
principle. It really starts, speaking in terms of logic,

by assuming the truth of its minor and takes for
granted that any major which will cover the
minor is therefore established. Nothing saves so
much trouble in thinking as the acceptance of a
good sounding generality or a self-evident truth.
Where your poor scientific worker plods along, testing the truth of his argument at every point, making
qualifications and reservations, and admitting that
every general principle may require to be modified in
concrete cases, you can thus both jump to your conclusion and assume the airs of a philosopher. It is,
I fancy, for this reason that people have such a
tendency to lay down absolute rules about really
difficult points. It is so much easier to say at once
that all drinking ought to be suppressed, than to
consider how, in actual circumstances, sobriety can
be judiciously encouraged; and by assuming a good
self-evident law and denouncing your opponents as
immoral worshippers of expediency, you place yourself in an enviable position of moral dignity and
inaccessibility. No argument can touch you. These
abstract rules, too, have the convenience of being
strangely ambiguous. I have been almost pathetic-
ally affected when I have observed how some
thoroughly commonplace person plumes himself on
preserving his consistency because he sticks resolutely
to his party dogmas, even when their whole meaning

has evaporated. Some English radicals boasted of consistency because they refused to be convinced by experience that republicans under a military dictator could become tyrannous and oppressive. At the present day, I see many worthy gentlemen, who from being thorough-going individualists, have come to swallow unconsciously the first principles of socialism without the least perception that they have changed, simply because a new meaning has been gradually insinuated into the sacred formulæ. Scientific habits of thought, I venture to suggest, would tend to free a man from the dominion of these abstract phrases, which sometimes make men push absolute dogmas to extravagant results, and sometimes blind them to the complete transformation which has taken place in their true meaning. The great test of statesmanship, it is said, is the knowledge how and when to make a compromise, and when to hold fast to a principle. The tendency of the thoughtless is to denounce all compromise as wicked, and to stick to a form of words without bothering about the real meaning. Belief in "fads"—I cannot avoid the bit of slang— and singular malleability of real convictions are sometimes generated just by want of serious thought; and, at any rate, both phenomena are very common at present.

This suggests another aspect of reasoning in a

scientific spirit, namely, the importance which it
attaches to a right comprehension of the practicable.
The scientific view is sometimes described as fatalistic. A genuine scientific theory implies a true
estimate of the great forces which mould institutions,
and therefore a true apprehension of the limits within
which they can be modified by any proposed change.
We all remember Sydney Smith's famous illustration,
in regard to the opposition to the Reform Bill, of
Mrs. Partington's attempt to stop the Atlantic with
her mop. Such an appeal is sometimes described as
immoral. Many politicians, no doubt, find in it an
excuse for immoral conduct. They assume that such
and such a measure is inevitable, and therefore they
think themselves justified for advocating it, even
though they hold it to be wrong. Indeed, I observe
that many excellent journalists are apparently unable
to perceive any distinction between the assertion
that a measure will be passed, and that it ought to
be passed. Undoubtedly, if I think a measure unjust,
I ought to say that it is unjust, even if I am sure
that it will nevertheless be carried, and, in some
cases, even though I may be a martyr to my opposition. If it is inevitable, it can be carried without my
help, and my protest may at least sow a seed for
future reaction. But this is no answer to the argument of Sydney Smith when taken in a reasonable

sense. The opposition to the Reform Bill was a particular case of the opposition to the advance of democracy. The statement that democracy has advanced and will advance, is sometimes taken to be fatalistic. People who make the assertion may answer for themselves. I should answer, as I think we should all answer now, that the advance of democracy, desirable or undesirable, depended upon causes far too deep and general to be permanently affected by any Reform Bill. It was only one aspect of vast social changes which had been going on for centuries; and to propose to stop it by throwing out the Reform Bill was like proposing to stop a child's growth by forcing him to go on wearing his long clothes. Sydney Smith's answer might be immoral if it simply meant, don't fight because you will be beaten. It may often be a duty to take a beating. But it was, perhaps, rather a way of saying that if you want to stop the growth of democracy, you must begin by altering the course of the social, intellectual and moral changes which have been operating through many generations, and that unless you can do that, it is idle to oppose one particular corollary, and so to make a revolution inevitable, instead of a peaceful development. To say that any change is impossible in the absolute sense, may be fatalism; but it is simple good sense, and therefore good

science, to say that to produce any change whatever
you must bring to bear a force adequate to the
change. When a man's leg is broken, you can't expect to heal it by a bit of sticking-plaster; a pill is
not supposed, now, to be a cure for an earthquake;
and to insist upon such facts is not to be fatalistic,
but simply to say that a remedy must bear some
proportion to an evil. It is a commonplace to observe
upon the advantage which would have been gained
if our grandfathers would have looked at the French
Revolution scientifically. A terrible catastrophe had
occurred abroad. The true moral, as we all see now,
was that England should make such reforms as
would obviate the danger of a similar catastrophe at
home. The moral which too many people drew was
too often, that all reforms should be stopped; with
the result that the evils grew worse and social strata
more profoundly alienated. It is a first principle of
scientific reasoning, that a break-down of social order
implies some antecedent defect, demanding an
adequate remedy. It is a primary assumption of
party argument, that the opposite party is wholly
wrong, that its action is perfectly gratuitous, and
either causeless or produced by the direct inspiration
of the devil. The struggle, upon the scientific theory,
represents two elements in an evolution which can be
accomplished peacefully by such a reconstruction as

will reconcile the conflicting aims and substitute harmony for discord. On the other doctrine, it is a conflict of hopelessly antagonistic principles, one of which is to be forcibly crushed.

I hope that I am not too sanguine, but I cannot help believing that in this respect we have improved, and improved by imbibing some of the scientific doctrine. I think that in recent discussions of the most important topics, however bitter and however much distorted by the old party spirit, there is yet a clearer recognition than of old, that widely-spread discontent is not a reason for arbitrary suppression, but for seeking to understand and remove its causes. We should act in the spirit of Spinoza's great saying; and it should be our aim, as it was his care, " neither to mock, to bewail, nor to denounce men's actions, but to understand them". That is equally true of men's opinions. If they are violent, passionate, subversive of all order, our duty is not bare denunciations, but a clear comprehension of the causes, not of the ostensible reasons, of their opinions, and a resolution to remove those causes. I think this view has made some way: I am sure that it will make more way if we become more scientific in spirit; and it is one of the main reasons for encouraging such a spirit. The most obvious difficulty just now is one upon which I must touch, though

with some fear and trembling. A terrible weapon
has lately been coming into perfection, to which its
inventors have given the elegant name of a "boom".
The principle is—so far as I can understand—that
the right frame of mind for dealing with the gravest
problems is to generate a state·of violent excitement, to adopt any remedy, real or supposed, which
suggests itself at the moment, and to denounce
everybody who suggests difficulties as a cynic or a
cold-blooded egoist; and therefore to treat grave
chronic and organic diseases of society by spasmodic
impulses, to make stringent laws without con-
descending to ask whether they will work, and try
the boldest experiments without considering whether
they are likely to increase or diminish the evil.
This, as some people think, is one of the inevitable
consequences of democracy. I hope that it is not; but
if it is, it is one of the inevitable consequences against
which we, as cultivators of science, should most
seriously protest, in the hope that we may some day
find Philip sober enough to consider the consequences
of his actions under the influence of spiritual intoxication. Professor Huxley, in one of those smart
passages of arms which so forcibly illustrated his
intellectual vigour, gave an apologue, which I wish
that I could steal without acknowledgment. He
spoke of an Irish carman who, on being told that he

was not going in the right direction, replied that he was at any rate going at a great pace. The scientific doctrine is simply that we should look at the map before we set out for Utopia; and I think that a doctrine which requires to be enforced by every means in our power.

This tendency, of course, comes out prominently in the important discussions of social and economic problems. That is a matter upon which I cannot now dwell, and which has been sufficiently emphasised by many eminent writers. If modern orators confined themselves to urging that the old economists exaggerated their claims to scientific accuracy, and were, in point of fact, guilty of many logical errors and hasty generalisations, I, at least, could fully agree with them. But the general impression seems to be, that because the old arguments were faulty, all argument is irrelevant: that because the alleged laws of nature were wrongly stated, there are no laws of nature at all; and that we may proceed to rearrange society, to fix the rate of wages or the rent of land or the incomes of capitalists without any reference at all to the conditions under which social arrangements have been worked out and actually carried on. This is, in short, to sanction the most obvious weakness of popular movements, and to assure the ignorant and thought-

less that they are above reason, and their crude
guesses infallible guides to truth.

One view which tries to give some plausibility to
these assumptions is summed up in the now current
phrase about the "masses" and the "classes". We
all know the regular process of logical fence of the
journalist, *i.e.*, thrust and parry, which is repeated
whenever such questions turn up. The Radical
calls his opponent Tory and reactionary. The
wicked Tory, it is said, thinks only of the class
interest; believes that the nation exists for the
sake of the House of Lords; lives in a little citadel
provided with all the good things, which he is ready
to defend against every attempt at a juster distribution; selfishness is his one motive; repression by
brute force his only theory of government; and
his views of life in general are those of the wicked
cynics who gaze from their windows in Pall Mall.
Then we have the roll of all the abuses which have
been defended by this miscreant and his like since
the days of George III.—slavery and capital punishment, and pensions and sinecures, and protection
and the church establishment. The popular instinct,
it is urged, has been in the right in so many cases
that there is an enormous presumption in favour of
the infallibility of all its instincts. The reply, of
course, is equally obvious. Your boast, says the

Conservative, that you please the masses, is in effect a confession that you truckle to the mob. You mean that your doctrines spread in proportion to the ignorance of your constituents. You prove the merits of your theories by showing that they disgust people the more they think. The Liberalism of a district, it has been argued, varies with the number of convictions for drunkenness. If it be easy to denounce our ancestors, it is also easy to show how they built up the great empire which now shelters us; and how, if they had truckled, as you would have us truckle, to popular whims, we should have been deprived of our commerce, our manufactures, and our position in the civilised world. And then it is easy to produce a list of all the base demagogues who have misled popular impatience and ignorance from the days of Cleon to those of the French Convention, or of the last disreputable " boss " bloated with corruption and the plunder of some great American city. This is the result, it is suggested, of pandering to the mob, and generally ostracising the intelligent citizen.

I merely sketch the familiar arguments which any journalist has ready at hand, and, by a sufficient spice of references to actual affairs, can work up into any number of pointed leading articles. I will only observe that such arguments seem to me to illustrate that curious unreality of political theories of which I have spoken. It seems to be tacitly assumed on both sides, that votes are determined by a process of genuine reasoning. One side may be ignorant and the other prejudiced; but the arguments I have recapitulated seem to imply the assumption that the constituents really reflect upon the reasons for and against the measures proposed, and make up their minds accordingly. They are spoken of as though they were a body of experts, investigating a scientific doctrine, or at least a jury guided by the evidence laid before them. Upon that assumption, as it seems to me, the moral would be that the whole system is a palpable absurdity. The vast majority of voters scarcely think at all, and would be incapable of judging if they did. Hundreds of thousands care more for Dr. Grace's last score or the winner of the Derby than for any political question whatever. If they have opinions, they have neither the training nor the knowledge necessary to form any conclusion whatever. Consider the state of mind of the average voter—of nine men out of ten, say, whom you meet in the Strand. Ask yourselves honestly what value you would attach to his opinion upon any great question—say, of foreign politics or political economy. Has he ever really thought about them? Is he superficially acquainted with any of the relevant facts? Is he even capable of the imaginative effort necessary to set before him the vast interests often affected? And would the simple fact that he said "Yes" to a given question establish in your mind the smallest presumption against the probability that the right answer would be "No"? What are the chances that a majority of people, of whom not one in a hundred has any qualifications for judging, will give a right judgment? Yet that is the test suggested by most of the conventional arguments on both sides; for I do not say this as intending to accept the anti-democratic application. It is just as applicable, I believe, to the educated and the well-off. I need not labour the point, which is sufficiently obvious. I am quite convinced that, for example, the voters for a university will be guided by unreasonable prejudices as the voters for a metropolitan constituency. In some ways they will be worse. To find people who believe honestly in antiquated prejudices, you must go to the people who have been trained to believe them. An ecclesiastical seminary can manage to drill the pupils into professing absurdities from which average common sense would shrink, and only supply logical machinery for warring against reason. The reference to enlightened aristocracies is common enough; but I cannot discover that, "taken in a lump," any particular aristocracy cannot be as narrow-minded, short-sighted, and selfish, as the most rampant democracy. In point of fact, we all know that political action is determined by instinct rather than by reason. I do not mean that instinct is opposed to reason: it is simply a crude, undeveloped, inarticulate form of reason; it is blended with prejudices for which no reason is assigned, or even regarded as requisite. Such blind instincts, implying at most a kind of groping after error, necessarily govern the majority of men of all classes, in political as in other movements. The old apologists used to argue on the hypothesis that men must have accepted Christianity on the strength of a serious inquiry into the evidences. The fallacy of the doctrine is sufficiently plain: they accepted it because it suited them on the whole, and was fitted, no doubt, to their intellectual needs, but was also fitted to their emotional and moral needs as developed under certain social conditions. The inference from the general acceptance of any theory is not that it is true, but that it is true enough to satisfy the very feeble demand for logic—that it is not palpably absurd or self-contradictory; and that, for some reason or other, it satisfies also the imagination, the affections, and the aspirations of the believers. Not to go into other questions, this

single remark indicates, I think, the attitude which
the scientific observer would adopt in regard to this
ancient controversy. He would study the causes as
well as the alleged reasons assignable for any general
instinct, and admit that its existence is one of the
primary data which have to be taken into account.
To denounce democracy or aristocracy is easy enough;
and it saves trouble to assume that God is on one
side and the devil on the other. The true method, I
take it, is that which was indicated by Tocqueville's
great book upon democracy in America; a book
which, if I may trust my own impressions, though
necessarily imperfect as regards America, is a
perfectly admirable example of the fruitful method of
studying such problems. Though an aristocrat by
birth and breeding, Tocqueville had the wisdom to
examine democratic beliefs and institutions in a
thoroughly impartial spirit ; and, instead of simply
denouncing or admiring, to trace the genesis of the
prevalent ideas and their close connection with the
general state of social development. An inquiry
conducted in that spirit would not lead to the absolute dogmatic conclusions in which the superficial
controversialist delights. It would show, perhaps,
that there was at least this much truth in the
democratic contention, that the masses are, by their
position, exempt from some of the prejudices which

are ingrained in the members of a smaller caste; that
they are therefore more accessible to certain moral
considerations, and more anxious to promote the
greatest happiness of the greater number. But it
might also show how the weakness of the ignorant
and untrained mind produces the characteristic evils
of sentimentalism and impatience, of a belief in the
omnipotence of legislation, and an excessive jealousy
of all superiorities; and might possibly, too, exhibit
certain merits which are impressed upon the aristocrat by his sense of the obligations of nobility. I do
not in the least mean to express any opinion about
such questions; I desire only to indicate the temper
in which I conceive that they should be approached.

I have lived long enough to be utterly unable to
believe—though some older politicians than I seem
still to believe, especially on the eve of a dissolution
—that any of our party lines coincide with the lines
between good and bad, wise and foolish. Every one,
of course, will repudiate the abstract theory. Yet we
may notice how constantly it is assumed; and can
see to what fallacies it leads when we look for a
moment at the historical questions which no longer
unite party feeling. Few, indeed, even of our
historians, can write without taking party views of
such questions. Even the candid and impartial seem
to deserve these epithets chiefly because they want

imagination, and can cast blame or applaud alter-
nately, because they do not enter into the real spirit
of either party. Their views are sometimes a medley
of inconsistent theories, rather than a deeper view
which might reconcile apparent inconsistencies. I will
only mention one point which often strikes me, and
may lead to a relevant remark. Every royalist
historian, we all know, labours to prove that Charles I.
was a saint, and Cromwell a hypocrite. The view was
natural at the time of the civil wars; but it now
should suggest an obvious logical dilemma. If the
monarchical theory which Charles represented was
sound, and Charles was also a wise and good man,
what caused the rebellion? A perfect man driving a
perfect engine should surely not have run it off the
rails. The royalist ought to seek to prove that
Charles was a fool and a knave, to account for the
collapse of royalty; and the case against royalty is
all the stronger, if you could show that Charles, in
spite of impeccable virtue, was forced by his position
to end on the scaffold. Choose between him and the
system which he applied. So Catholics and conservatives are never tired of denouncing Henry VIII.
and the French revolutionists. So far as I can guess
(I know very little about it), their case is a very
strong one. I somehow believe, in spite of Froude,
that Henry VIII. was a tyrant; and eulogies upon

the reign of terror generally convince me that a greater set of scoundrels seldom came to the surface, than the perpetrators of those enormities. But then the real inference is, to my mind, very different. Henry VIII. was the product of the previous time; the ultimate outcome of that ideal state of things in which the church had its own way during the ages of truth. Must not the system have been wrong, when it had so lost all moral weight as to be at the mercy of a ruffianly plunderer? And so, as we all admit now, the strongest condemnation of the old French *régime* is the fact that it had not only produced such a set of miscreants as those who have cast permanent odium even upon sound principles; but that its king and rulers went down before them without even an attempt at manly resistance. A revolution does not, perhaps, justify itself; it does not prove that its leaders judged rightly and acted virtuously: but, beyond a doubt, it condemns the previous order which brought it about. What a horrid thing is the explosion! Why, is the obvious answer, did you allow the explosive materials to accumulate, till the first match must fire the train? The greatest blot upon Burke, I need hardly say, is that his passions blinded him in his age, to this, as we now see, inevitable conclusion.

The old-fashioned view, I fancy, is a relic of that

view of history in which all the great events and changes were personified in some individual hero. The old "legislators," Lycurgus and Solon and the like, were supposed to have created the institutions which were really the products of a slow growth. When a favourable change due to economical causes took place in the position of the French peasantry, the peasants, says Michelet somewhere, called it "good king Henry". Carlyle's theory of hero worship is partly an application of the same mode of thought. You embody your principle in some concrete person; canonise him or damn him, as he represents truth or error; and take credit to yourself for insight and for a lofty morality. It becomes a kind of blasphemy to suggest that your great man, who thus stands for an inspired leader dropped straight out of heaven, was probably at best very imperfect, one-sided, and at least as much of a product as a producer. The crudity of the method is even regarded as a proof of its morality. Your common-place moralist likes to call everything black or white; he despises all qualifications as casuistical refinements, and plumes himself on the decisive verdict, saint or sinner, with which he labels the adherents and opponents of his party. And yet we know as a fact, how absurd are such judgments. We know how men are betrayed into bad causes from good motives, or put on the right side because

it happens to harmonise with their lower interests.
Saints—so we are told—have been the cruellest per-
secutors; and kings, acting from purely selfish
ambition, have consolidated nations or crushed effete
and mischievous institutions.   If we can make up
our minds as to which was, on the whole, the best
cause,—and, generally speaking, both sides represented some sound principle,—it does not follow that
it was also the cause of all the best men.   Before we
can judge of the individual, we must answer a
hundred difficult questions: If he took the right side,
did he take it from the right motives?   Was it from
personal ambition or pure patriotism?   Did he see
what was the real question at issue?   Did he foresee
the inevitable effect of the measures which he advocated?   If he did not see, was it because he was
human, and therefore short-sighted; or because he
was brutal, and therefore wanting in sympathy; or
because he had intellectual defects, which made it
impossible for him to escape from the common
illusions of the time?   These, and any number of
similar difficulties, arise when we try to judge of the
great men who form landmarks in our history, from
the time of Boadicea to that of Queen Victoria.
They are always amusing, and sometimes important;
but there is always a danger that they may warp our
views of the vital facts.   The beauty of Mary Queen

of Scots still disqualifies many people from judging
calmly the great issues of a most important historical
epoch.   I will leave it to you to apply this to our
views of modern politics, and judge the value of the
ordinary assumption which assumes that all good
men must be on one side.

Now we may say that the remedy for such illusions points to the importance of a doctrine which is
by no means new, but which has, I think, bearings
not always recognised.   We have been told, again and
again, since Plato wrote his *Republic*, that society is
an organism.   It is replied that this is at best an
analogy upon which too great stress must not be
laid ; and we are warned against the fanciful com-
parisons which some writers have drawn between
the body corporate and the actual physical body,
with its cells, tissues, nervous system, and so forth.
Now, whatever may be the danger of that mode of
reasoning, I think that the statement, properly
understood, corresponds to a simple logical canon
too often neglected in historical and political reasonings.   It means, I take it, in the first place, that
every man is a product as well as a producer; that
there is no such thing as the imaginary individual
with fixed properties, whom theorists are apt to take
for granted as the base of their reasoning; that no
man or group of men is intelligible without taking

into account the mass of instincts transmitted
through their predecessors, and therefore without
referring to their position in the general history of
human development. And, secondly, it is essential
to remember in speaking of any great man, or of any
institution, their position as parts of a complicated
system of actions and emotions. The word "if," I
may say, changes its meaning. "If" Harold had
won the battle of Hastings, what would have been
the result? The answer would be comparatively
simple, if we could, in the old fashion, attribute to
William the Conqueror all the results in which he
played a conspicuous part: if, therefore, we could
make out a definite list of effects of which he was
the cause, and, by simply "deducting" them, after
Coleridge's fashion, from the effects which actually
followed, determine what was the precise balance.
But when we consider how many causes were
actually in operation, how impossible it is to disentangle and separate them, and say this followed
from that, and that other from something else, we
have to admit that the might have been is simply
indiscoverable. The great man may have hastened
what was otherwise inevitable; he may simply have
supplied the particular point, round which a crystal-
lisation took place of forces which would have otherwise discovered some other centre; and the fact

that he succeeded in establishing certain institutions
or laws may be simply a proof that he saw a little
more clearly than others the direction towards which
more general causes were inevitably propelling the
nation. Briefly, we cannot isolate the particular
"cause" in this case, and have to remember at every
moment that it was only one factor in a vast and
complex series of changes, which would no doubt
have taken a different turn without it, but of which
it may be indefinitely difficult to say what was the
precise deflection due to its action.

In trying to indicate the importance, I have had
to dwell upon the difficulty, of applying anything
like scientific methods to political problems. I shall
conclude by trying once more to indicate why, in
spite of this, I hold that the attempt is desirable, and
may be fruitful.

People sometimes say that scientific methods are
inapplicable because we cannot try experiments in
social matters. I remember being long ago struck
by a remark of Dr. Arnold, which has some bearing
upon this assertion. He observed upon the great
advantage possessed by Aristotle in the vast number
of little republics in his time, each of which was
virtually an experiment in politics. I always thought
that this was fallacious somehow, and I fancy that it
is not hard to indicate the general nature of the

fallacy. Freeman, upon whose services to thorough
and accurate study of history I am unworthy to pronounce an eulogy, fell into the same fallacy, I fancy,
when he undertook to write a history of Federal
Governments. He fancied that because the Achæan
League and the Swiss Cantons and the United States
of America all had this point in common, and that
they represented the combinations of partially independent States, their history would be in a sense
continuous. The obvious consideration that the
federations differed in every possible way, in their
religions and state of civilisation and whole social
structure, might be neglected. Freeman's tendency
to be indifferent to everything which was not in the
narrowest sense political led him to this—as it
seems to me—pedantic conception. If the prosperity of a nation depended exclusively upon the
form of its government, Aristotle, as Arnold remarks, would have had before him a greater number
of experiments than the modern observer. But the
assumption is obviously wrong. Every one of these
ancient States depended for its prosperity upon a
vast number of conditions—its race, its geographical
position, its stage of development, and so forth, quite
impossible to tabulate or analyse; and the form of
government which suited one would be entirely inapplicable to another. To extricate from all these

conflicting elements the precise influence due to any
institutions would be a task beyond the powers of
any number of philosophers; and indeed the per-
plexity would probably be increased by the very
number of experiments. To make an experiment
fruitful, it is necessary to eliminate all the irrelevant
elements which intrude into the concrete cases spontaneously offered by nature, and, for example, to
obtain two cases differing only in one element, to
which we may therefore plausibly attribute other
contrasts. Now, the history of a hundred or a
thousand small States would probably only present
the introduction of new and perplexing elements for
every new case. The influence, again, of individuals,
or accident of war, or natural catastrophes, is
greater in proportion as the State is smaller, and
therefore makes it more difficult to observe the permanent and underlying influences. It seems to me,
therefore, that the study, say of English history,
where we have a continuous growth over many
centuries, where the disturbing influences of individuals or chance are in a greater degree cancelled by
the general tendencies working beneath them, we
have really a far more instructive field for political
observation. This may help us to see what are the
kinds of results which may be anticipated from sociological study undertaken in a serious spirit. The

growth, for example, of the industrial system of England is a profoundly interesting subject of inquiry,
to which we are even now only beginning to do
justice.   Historians have admitted, even from the
time of Hume, that the ideal history should give less
of mere battles and intrigues, and more account of
those deeper and more continuous processes which
lie, so to speak, beneath the surface.   They have
hardly, I think, even yet realised the full bearing and
importance of this observation.   Yet, of late, much
has been done, though much still remains to do, in
the way of a truly scientific study of the development of institutions, political, ecclesiastical, industrial, and so forth, of this and other countries.   As
this tendency grows, we may hope gradually to have
a genuine history of the English people ; an account
—not of the virtues and vices of Mary Queen of
Scots, or arguments as to the propriety of cutting off
Charles I.'s head—but a trustworthy account of the
way in which the actual structure of modern society
has been developed out of its simpler germs.   The
biographies of great kings and generals, and so forth,
will always be interesting ; but to the genuine historian of the future they will be interesting not so
much as giving room for psychological analyses or
for dramatic portraits, but as indications of the great
social forces which produced them, and the direction

of which at the moment may be illustrated by their cases. I have spoken of the history of our industrial system. To know what was the position of the English labourer at various times, how it was affected by the political changes or by the great mechanical discoveries, to observe what grievances arose, what remedies were applied or sought to be applied, and with what result,—to treat all this with due reference to the whole social and intellectual evolution of which it formed a part, may well call forth the powers of our acutest and most thoroughgoing inquirers, and will, when it is done, give essential data for some of the most vitally important problems of the day. This is what I understand by an application of the scientific spirit to social and political problems. We cannot try experiments, it is said, in historical questions. We cannot help always trying experiments, and experiments of vast importance. Every man has to try an experiment upon himself when he chooses his career; and the results are frequently very unpleasant, though very instructive. We have to be our own experiments. Every man who sets up in business tries an experiment, ending in fortune or in bankruptcy. Every strike is an experiment, and generally a costly one. Every attempt at starting a new charitable organisation, or a new system of

socialism or co-operation, is an experiment. Every
new law is an experiment, rash or otherwise. And
from all these experiments we do at least collect
a certain number of general observations, which,
though generally consigned to copybooks, are not
without value. What is true, however, is that we
cannot try such experiments as a man of science can
sometimes try in his laboratory, where he can select
and isolate the necessary elements in any given process, and decide, by subjecting them to proper
conditions, how a definite question is to be answered.
Our first experiments are all in the rough, so to
speak, tried at haphazard, and each involving an indefinite number of irrelevant conditions. But there
is a partial compensation. We cannot tabulate the
countless experiments which have been tried with
all their distracting varieties. Yet in a certain sense
the answer is given for us. For the social structure
at any period is in fact the net product of all the
experiments that have been made by the individuals
of which it is and has been composed. Therefore,
so far as we can obtain some general views of the
successive changes in social order which have
been gradually and steadily developing themselves
throughout the more noisy and conspicuous but comparatively superficial political disturbances, we can
detect the true meaning of some general phenomena

in which the actors themselves were unconscious of the determining causes. We can see more or less what were the general causes which have led to various forms of associations, to the old guilds, or the modern factory system, to the trades unions or the co-operative societies ; and correcting and verifying our general results by a careful examination of the particular instances, approximate, vaguely it may be and distantly, to some such conception of the laws of development of different social tissues as, if not properly scientific, may yet belong to the scientific order of thought. Thus, when distracted by this or that particular demand, by promises of the millennium to be inaugurated to-morrow by an Act of Parliament, or threats of some social cataclysm to overwhelm us if we concede an inch to wicked agitators, we may succeed in placing ourselves at a higher point of view, from which it is possible to look over wider horizons, to regard what is happening to-day in its relations to slow processes of elaboration, and to form judgments based upon wide and systematic inquiry, which, if they do not entitle us to predict particular events, as an astronomer predicts an eclipse, will at least be a guide to sane and sober minds, and suggest at once a humbler appreciation of what is within our power, and—I think also—a more really hopeful anticipation of genuine progress in the future.

All scientific inquiry is an interrogation of nature. We have, in Bacon's grand sententious phrase, to command nature by obeying. We learn what are the laws of social growth by living them. The great difficulty of the interrogation is to know what questions we are to put. Under the guidance of metaphysicians, we have too often asked questions to which no answer is conceivable, like children, who in first trying to think, ask, why are we living in the nineteenth century, why is England an island, or why does pain hurt, or why do two and two make four? The only answer is by giving the same facts in a different set of words, and that is a kind of answer to which metaphysical dexterity sometimes gives an air of plausibility. More frequently our ingenuity takes the form of sanctioning preconceived prejudices, by wrapping up our conclusion in our premisses, and then bringing it out triumphantly with the air of a rigorous deduction. The progress of social science implies, in the first place, the abandonment of the weary system of hunting for fruitful truths in the region of chimeras, and trying to make empty logical concepts do the work of observation of facts. It involves, again, a clear perception of the kind of questions which can be profitably asked, and the limits within which an answer, not of the illusory kind, can really be expected. And then we may

come to see that, without knowing it, we have really
been trying a vast and continuous experiment, since
the race first began to be human. We have, blindly
and unconsciously, constructed a huge organism
which does, somehow or other, provide a great many
millions of people with a tolerable amount of food
and comfort. We have accomplished this, I say,
unconsciously; for each man, limited to his own
little sphere, and limited to his own interests, and
guided by his own prejudices and passions, has been
as ignorant of more general tendencies as the coral
insect of the reef which it has helped to build. To
become distinctly conscious of what it is that we
have all been doing all this time, is one step in advance. We have obeyed in ignorance; and as
obedience becomes conscious, we may hope, within
certain narrow limits, to command, or, at least, to
direct. An enlarged perception of what have been
the previous results may enable us to see what results are possible, and among them to select what
may be worthy ends. It is not to be supposed that
we shall ever get beyond the need of constant and
careful experiment. But, in proportion as we can
cultivate the right frame of mind, as each member
of society requires wider sympathies and a larger
horizon, it is permissible to hope that the experiments may become more intelligent; that we shall

not, as has so often been done, increase poverty by
the very remedies which are intended to remove it,
or diverge from the path of steady progressive
development, into the chase of some wild chimera,
which requires for its achievement only the radical
alteration of all the data of experience. " Annihilate
space and time, and make two lovers happy," was
the modest petition of an enthusiast ; and he would
probably have been ready to join in the prayer, "make
all men angels, and then we shall have a model
society ". Although in saying this my immediate
moral is to preach sobriety, I do not intend to denounce enthusiasm, but to urge a necessity of
organising enthusiasm. I only recommend people
not to venture upon flying machines before they have
studied the laws of mechanics ; but I earnestly hope
that some day we may be able to call a balloon as
we now call a cab. To point out the method, and to
admit that it is not laborious, is not to discourage
aspiration, but to look facts in the face : not to preach
abandonment of enthusiasm, but to urge that enthusiasm should be systematic, should lead men to
study the conditions of success, and to make a bridge
before they leap the gulf.

THE SPHERE OF POLITICAL ECONOMY.

THERE seem to be at present many conflicting views as to the nature of Political Economy. There is a popular impression that Political Economy, or, at any rate, the so-called "classical" doctrine, the doctrine which was made most definite by Ricardo, and accepted with modifications by J. S. Mill, is altogether exploded. Their main doctrines, it is suggested, were little better than mares' nests, and we may set aside their pretensions to have founded an exact science. What, then, is to come in its place? Are we simply to admit that there is no certainty about economical problems, and to fall back upon mere empiricism? Everything,—shall we say?— is to be regarded as an open question. That is, perhaps, a common impression in the popular mind. Yet, on the other hand, we may find some very able thinkers applying mathematical formulæ to economics; and that seems to suppose, that within a certain region they obtain results comparable in precision and accuracy to those of the great physical sciences. The topic is a very wide one; and it would

be presumptuous in me to speak dogmatically.   I
wish, however, to suggest certain considerations
which may, perhaps, be worth taking into account;
and, as I must speak briefly, I must not attempt to
supply all the necessary qualifications.   I can only
attempt to indicate what seems to me to be the
correct point of view, and apologise if I appear to
speak too dogmatically, simply because I cannot
waste time by expressions of diffidence, by reference
to probable criticisms, or even by a full statement of
my own reasons.

A full exposition would have to define the sphere
of Political Economy by describing its data and its
methods.   What do we assume, and how do we
reason? A complete answer to these questions would
indicate the limits within which we can hope for valid
conclusions.   I will first refer, briefly, to a common
statement of one theory advocated by the old-
fashioned or classical school.   Economic doctrine,
they have said, supposes a certain process of abstraction.   We have to do with what has been called the
"economic man". He is not, happily, the real man.
He is an imaginary being, whose sole principle of
action is to buy in the cheapest and sell in the dearest market: a man, more briefly, who always prefers
a guinea—even a dirty guinea—to a pound of the
cleanest.   Economists reply to the remonstrances of

those who deny the existence of such a monster, by adding that they do not for a moment suppose that men in general, or even tradesmen or stockbrokers, are in reality such beings,—mere money-making machines, stripped bare of all generous or altruistic sentiment—but simply that, as a matter of fact, most people do, *ceteris paribus*, prefer a guinea to a pound ; and that so large a part of our industrial activity is carried on from motives of this kind, that we may obtain a fair approximation to the actual course of affairs by considering them as the sole motives. We shall not go wrong, for example, in financial questions, by assuming that the sole motive of speculators in the Stock Exchange is the desire to make money.   Now, it is possible, perhaps, to justify this way of putting the case, by certain qualifications.   I think, however, that, if strictly interpreted, it is apt to cover a serious fallacy.   The "economic man" theory, we may say, assumes too much in one direction, and too little in another.   It assumes too much if it is understood as implying that the desire for wealth is a purely selfish desire.   A man may desire to make money in order simply to gratify his own sensual appetites.   But he may also desire to be independent ; and that may include a desire to do his part in the work of society, and probably does include some desire to relieve others of a burden.   The wish

to be self-supporting is not necessarily or purely
" selfish ".   And obviously, too, one great motive in
all such occupations is the desire to support a family,
and one main inducement to saving is the desire to
support it after your own death.   Remove such
motives, and half the impulses to regular industrial
energy of all kinds would be destroyed.   We must,
therefore, give our "economic man" credit for motives
referring to many interests besides those which he
buttons into his own waistcoat.   And therefore, too,
as I have said, the assumption it insufficient.   The
very conception of economic science supposes all that
is supposed, in the growth of a settled order of
society.   The purest type of the " economic man,"
as he is sometimes described, would be realised in
the lowest savage, as sometimes described, who is
absolutely selfish, who knocks his child on the head
because it cries, and eats his aged parent if he cannot find a supply of roots.   But such a being could
only form herds, not societies.   Political Economy
only becomes conceivable when we suppose certain
institutions to have been developed.   It assumes,
obviously, and in the first place, the institution of
property; it becomes applicable, with less qualification, in proportion to the growth of the corresponding sentiments; it takes for granted all that
highly elaborate set of instincts which induce me,

when I want something, to produce an equivalent in exchange for it, instead of going out to take it by force. The more thorough the respect for property, the more applicable are rules of economics; and that respect implies a long training in that sense of other people's rights, which, unfortunately, is by no means so perfect as might be desired.

It follows, then, that the economist really assumes more—and rightly assumes more—than he sometimes claims. He assumes what Adam Smith assumed at the opening of his great treatise : that is, the division of labour.   But the division of labour implies the organisation of society.   It implies that one man is growing corn while another is digging gold, because each is confident that he will be able to exchange the products of his own labour for the products of the other man's labour.   This, of course, implies settled order, respect for contracts, the preservation of peace, and the abolition of force throughout the area occupied by the society.   And this, again, is only possible in so far as certain political and ecclesiastical and military institutions have been definitely constructed.   The economic assumption is really an assumption—not of a certain psychological condition of the average man, but—of the existence of a certain social mechanism.   A complete science would clear up fully a problem

which must occur often to all of us: How do you
account for London? How is it that four or five
millions of people manage to subsist on an area of
a few square miles, which itself produces nothing?
that other millions all over the world are engaged in
providing for their wants? that food and clothes and
fuel, in sufficient quantities to preserve life, are being
distributed with tolerable regularity to each unit in
this vast and apparently chaotic crowd? and that,
somehow or other, we struggle on, well or ill, by the
help of a gigantic commissariat, performing functions
incomparably more complex than were ever needed
for military purposes? The answer supposes that
there is, as a matter of fact, a great industrial
organisation which discharges the various functions
of producing, exchanging, distributing, and so forth;
and that its mutual relations are just as capable
of being investigated and stated as the relations between different parts of an army. The men and
officers do not wear uniforms; they are not explicitly
drilled or subject to a definite code of discipline; and
their rates of pay are not settled by any central
authority. But there are capitalists, "undertakers"
and labourers, merchants and retail dealers and con-
tractors, and so forth, just as certainly as there are
generals and privates, horse, foot, and artillery; and
their mutual relations are equally definable. The

economist has to explain the working of this industrial mechanism ; and the thought may sometimes
occur to us, that it is strange that he should find the
task so difficult. Since we ourselves have made, or
at any rate constitute, the mechanism, why should it
be so puzzling to find out what it is ? We are co-
operating in a systematic production and distribution
of wealth, and we surely ought not to find any
impenetrable mystery in discovering what it is that
we are doing every day of our lives. Certain
economists writing within this century have often
been credited with the discovery of the true theory
of rent, or, which is equally good for my purpose, of
starting a false theory. Yet landowners and agents
had been letting farms and houses for generations ;
and surely they ought to have known what it was
that they were themselves doing. One explanation
of the difficulty is, that whereas an army is constituted by certain regulations of a central authority,
the industrial army has grown up unconsciously and
spontaneously. Its multitudinous members have
only looked each at his own little circle ; the
labourer only thinks of his wages, and the capitalist
of his profits, without considering his relations to the
whole system of which he forms a part. The
peasant drives his plough for wages, and buys his
tea as if the tea fell like manna from the skies, with-

out thinking of the curious relation into which he is thus brought with the natives of another hemisphere. The order which results from all these independent activities appeared to the older economists as an illustration of the doctrine of Final Causes. Providence had so ordered things that each man, by pursuing his own interests, pursued the interests of all. To a later school it appears rather as an illustration of the doctrine by which organisms are constructed through the struggle for existence and the survival of the fittest. In either case, it seems as though the mechanism were made rather for us than by us; that it is the product of conditions which we cannot control, instead of being an arrangement put together by conscious volitions. And, therefore, when the economist shows us what in fact are the existing arrangements and their mutual relations, he appears to be making a discovery of a scientific fact as much as if he were describing the anatomy of some newly-discovered animal or plant.

The real assumption of the economist therefore is, as I think, simply the existence of a certain industrial organisation, which has a real existence as much as an army or a church; and there is no reason why his description should not be as accurate as the complexity of the facts allows. He is giving us the anatomy of society considered as a huge mechanism

for producing and distributing wealth, and he makes
an abstraction only in the sense that he is considering one set of facts at a time. The military writer
would describe the constitution of an army without
going into the psychological or political conditions
which are of course implied, and without considering
the soldiers in any other relations than those implied
in their military services.   In the same way, the
economist describes the army of industry, and
classifies its constituent parts. In order to explain
their mutual relations, he has to make certain
further assumptions, of which it would be rash to
attempt a precise summary. He assumes as a fact,
what has of course always been known, that scarcity
implies dearness and plenty cheapness; that commodities flow to the markets where they will fetch
the highest prices; that there is a certain gravitation
towards equalisation of profits among capitalists, and
of wages among labourers; so that capital or labour
will flow towards the employments in which they
will secure the highest reward. He endeavours to
give the greatest accuracy to such formulæ, of which
nobody, so far as I know, denies a certain approximate truth.   So long as they hold good, his
inferences, if logically drawn, will also hold good.
They take for granted certain psychological facts,
such as are implied in all statements about human

nature.   But the economist, as an economist, is
content to take them for granted without investigating the ultimate psychological laws upon which
they depend.   Those laws, or rather their results,
are a part of his primary data, although he may go
so far into psychological problems as to try to state
them more accurately.   The selfishness or unselfish-
ness of the economic man has to be considered by
the psychologist or by the moralist; but the economist has only to consider their conclusions so far as
they affect the facts.   So long as it is true, for
example, that scarcity causes dearness, that profits
attract capital, that demand and supply tend to
equalise each other, and so forth, his reasonings are
justified; and the further questions of the ethical and
psychological implications of these facts must be
treated by a different science.   The question of the
play of economic forces thus generally reduces itself
to a problem which may be thus stated : What are
the conditions of industrial equilibrium ?   How must
prices, rates of wages, and profit be related in order
that the various classes concerned may receive such
proportions of produce as are compatible with the
maintenance of the existing system of organisation ?
If any specified change occurs, if production becomes
easier or more difficult, if a tax be imposed, or
a regulation of any kind affects previous conditions,

what changes will be necessary to restore the equilibrium? These are the main problems of Political
Economy. To solve, or attempt to solve them, we
have to describe accurately the existing mechanism,
and to suppose that it will regulate itself on the
assumption which I have indicated as to demand
and supply, the flow of capital and labour, and so
forth. To go beyond these assumptions, and to
justify them by psychological and other considerations, may be and is a most interesting task, but it
takes us beyond the sphere of Economics proper.

I must here diverge for a little, to notice the view
of the school of economists which seems to regard
scientific accuracy as attainable by a different path.
Jevons, its most distinguished leader in England,
says roundly, that political science must be a
"mathematical science," because "it deals throughout with quantities"; and we have been since provided with a number of formulæ, corresponding to
this doctrine. The obvious general reply would be,
that Political Economy cannot be an exact science
because it also deals throughout with human desires.
The objection is not simply that our data are too
vague. That objection, as Jevons says, would, perhaps, apply to meteorology, of which nobody doubts
that it is capable of being made an exact science.
But why does nobody doubt that meteorology might

become an exact science ?   Because we are convinced that all the data which would be needed are
expressible in precise terms of time and space; we
have to do with volumes, and masses, and weights,
and forces which can be exactly measured by lines;
and, in short, with things which could be exactly
measured and counted.   The data are, at present,
insufficiently known, and possibly the problems which
would result might be too complex for our powers of
calculation.   Still, if we could once get the data, we
could express all relevant considerations by precise
figures and numbers.

Now, is this true of economic science?   Within
certain limits, it is apparently true : Ricardo used
mathematical formulæ, though he kept to arithmetic,
instead of algebra.   When Malthus spoke of arithmetical and geometrical ratios, the statement, true or
false, was, of course, capable of precise numerical expression, so soon as the ratios were assigned.   So
there was the famous formula proving a relation between the number of quarters of corn produced by a
given harvest, and the number of shillings that would
be given for a quarter of corn.   If, again, we took the
number of marriages corresponding to a given price
of corn, we should obtain a formula connecting the
number of marriages with the number of quarters of
corn produced.   The utility of statistics, of course,

depends upon the fact that we do empirically discover some tolerably constant and simple numerical
formulæ. Such statistical statements are useful, indeed, not only in economical, but in other inquiries,
which are clearly beyond the reach of mathematics.
The proportion of criminals in a given population,
the number of suicides, or of illegitimate births, may
throw some light upon judicial and political, and
even religious or ethical problems.   Nor are such
formulæ useless simply because empirical.   The law
of gravitation, for example, is empirical.   Nobody
knows the cause of the observed tendency of bodies
to gravitate to each other, and therefore no one can
say how far the law which represents the tendency
must be universal.   Still, the fact that, so far as we
have observed, it is invariably verified, and that
calculations founded upon it enable us to bring a vast
variety of phenomena under a single rule, is quite
enough to justify astronomical calculation.

If, therefore, we could find a mathematical formula
which was, as a matter of fact, verifiable in economical problems about prices, and so forth, we
should rightly apply to mathematicians to help us
with their methods.   But, not only do we not find
any such simple relations, but we can see conclusive
reasons for being sure that we can never find them.
Take, for example, the case of the number of

marriages under given conditions. I need hardly say that it is impossible for the ablest mathematician to calculate whether the individual A will marry the individual B. But, by taking averages, and so eliminating individual eccentricities, he might discover that, in a given country and at a given time, a rise of prices will diminish marriages in certain proportion. Our knowledge of human nature is sufficient to make that highly probable. But our knowledge also shows that such a change will act differently in different cases: there will be one formula for France, and another for England; one for Lancashire, and another for Cornwall; one for the rich, and another for the poor; and both the total wealth of a country and its distribution will affect the rule. Differences of national temperament, of political and social constitution, of religion and ecclesiastical organisation, will all have an effect; and, therefore, a formula true here and now must, in all probability, fail altogether elsewhere. The formula is, in the mathematical phrase, a function of so many independent variables, that it must be complex beyond all conception, if it takes them all into account; while it must yet be necessarily inaccurate if it does not take them into account. But, besides this, the conditions upon which the law obviously depends are not themselves capable of being accurately defined, and still less of being numerically stated. Ingenious thinkers have, indeed, tried to apply mathematical formulæ to psychology ; but they have not got very far ; and it may, I think, be assumed, without further argument, that while you have to deal both with psychological and sociological elements, with human desires, and with those desires modified by social relations, it is impossible to find any data which can be mathematically stated. There is no arithmetical measure of the forces of love, or hunger, or avarice, by which (among others) the whole problem is worked out.

It seems to me, therefore, that we must accept the alternative which is only mentioned to be repudiated by Jevons, namely, that Political Economy, if not a "mathematical science," must be part of sociology. I should say that it clearly is so ; for if we wish to investigate the cause of any of the phenomena concerned, and not simply to tabulate from observations, we are at once concerned with the social structure and with the underlying psychology. The mathematical methods are quite in their place when dealing with statistics. The rise and fall of prices, and so forth, can be stated precisely in figures ; and, whenever we can discover some approximation to a mathematical law (as in the cases I have noticed) we may work out the results. If, for example, the price of a commodity under

certain conditions bears a certain relation to its
scarcity, we can discover the one fact when the other
fact is given, remembering only that our conclusions
are not more certain than our premisses, and that
the observed law depends upon unknown and most
imperfectly knowable conditions. Such results, again,
may be very useful in various ways, as illustrative of
the way in which certain laws will work if they hold
good; and, again, as testing many of our general
theories.   If you have argued that the price of gold
or silver cannot be fixed, the fact that it has been
fixed under certain conditions will of course lead to
a revision of your arguments.   But I cannot help
thinking that it is an illusion to suppose that
such methods can justify the assertion that the
science as a whole is "mathematical".   Nothing,
indeed, is easier than to speak as if you had got a
mathematical theory.   Let x mean the desire for
marriage and y the fear of want, then the number of
marriages is a function of x and y, and I can express
this by symbols as well as by ordinary words.   But
there is no magic about the use of symbols.   Mathematical inquiries are not fruitful because symbols are
used, but because the symbols represent something
absolutely precise and assignable.   The highest
mathematical inquiries are simply ingenious methods
of counting; and till you have got something precise

to count, they can take you no further. I cannot
help thinking that this fallacy imposes upon some
modern reasoners ; that they assume that they have
got the data because they have put together the
formulæ which would be useful if they had the data ;
and, in short, that you can get more out of a mill
than you put into it ; or, in other words, that more
conclusions than really follow can be got out of
premisses, simply because you show what would
follow if you had the required knowledge. When
the attempt is made, as it seems to me to be made
sometimes, to deduce economical laws from some
law of human desire—as from the simple theorem
that equal increments of a commodity imply diminishing amounts of utility—I should reply not
only that the numerical data are vaguely defined and
incapable of being accurately stated, but that the
attempt must be illusory because the conclusions are
not determinable from the premisses. The economic
laws do not follow from any simple rule about
human desires, because they vary according to the
varying constitution of human society ; and any conclusion which you could obtain would be necessarily
confined to the abstract man of whom the law is supposed to hold good. Every such method, therefore,
if it could be successful, could only lead to conclusions about human desire in general, and could

throw no light upon the special problems of political economy, which essentially depend upon varying industrial organisation.

I will not, however, go further. You must either, I hold, limit Political Economy to the field of statistical inquiry, or admit that, as a part of sociology, it deals with questions altogether beyond the reach of mathematics. Like physiology, it is concerned with results capable of numerical statement. The number of beats of the pulse, or the number of degrees of temperature of the body, are important data in physiological problems. They may be counted, and may give rise to mathematically expressible formulæ. But the fact does not excuse us from considering the physical conditions of the organs which are in some way correlated with these observed phenomena; and, in the case of Political Economy, we have to do with the social structure, which is dependent upon forces altogether incapable of precise numerical estimates. That, at least, is my view; and I shall apply it to illustrate one remark, which must, I think, have often occurred to us. Political Economy, that is, often appears to have a negative rather than a positive value. It is exceedingly potent—so, at least, I think—in dispersing certain popular fallacies; but it fails when we regard it as a science which can give us positive concrete "laws". The general reason

is, I should say, that although its first principles
may be true descriptions of facts, and any denial of
them, or any inconsistent applications of them, may
lead us into error, they are yet far from sufficient
descriptions. They omit some considerations which
are relevant in any concrete case; and the facts
which they describe are so complex that, even when
we look at them consistently and follow the right
clue, we cannot solve the complicated problems
which occur. It may be worth while to insist a little
upon this, and to apply it to one or two peculiar
problems.

Let me start from the ordinary analogy. Economic
inquiry, I have suggested, describes a certain existing
mechanism, which exists as really as the physical
structure described by an anatomist. The industrial
organism has, of course, many properties of which
the economist, as such, does not take account. The
labourer has affections, and imaginations, and
opinions outside of his occupation as labourer; he
belongs to a state, a church, a family, and so forth,
which affect his whole life, including his industrial
life. Is it therefore impossible to consider the industrial organisation separately? Not more impossible, I should reply, than to apply the same
method in regard to the individual body. Were I to
regard my stomach simply as a bag into which I put

my food, I should learn very little about the process
of digestion. Still, it is such a bag, and it is important to know where it is, and what are its purely
mechanical relations to other parts of the body. My
arms and legs are levers, and I can calculate the
pressure necessary to support a weight on the hand,
as though my bones and muscles were made of iron
and whipcord. I am a piece of mechanism, though
I am more, and all the principles of simple
mechanics apply to my actions, though they do not,
by themselves, suffice to explain the actions. The
discovery of the circulation of the blood explained,
as I understand, my structure as a hydraulic ap-
paratus ; and it was of vast importance, even though
it told us nothing directly of the other processes
necessarily involved. In this case, therefore, we
have an instance of the way in which a set of perfectly
true propositions may, so to speak, be imbedded in a
larger theory, and may be of the highest importance,
though they are not by themselves sufficient to solve
any concrete problem. We cannot, that is, deduce
the physiological principles from the mechanical
principles, although they are throughout implied.
But those principles are not the less true and useful
in the detection of fallacies. They may enable us to
show that an argument supposes facts which do not
exist ; or, perhaps, that it is, at any rate, inconsistent

because it assumes one structure in its premisses, and another in its conclusions.

I state this by way of illustration: but the value of the remark may be best tested by applying it to some economical doctrines. Let us take, for example, the famous argument of Adam Smith against what he called the mercantile theory. That theory, according to him, supposed that the wealth of nations, like the wealth of an individual, was in proportion to the amount of money in their possession. He insisted upon the theory that money, as it is useful solely for exchange, cannot be, in itself, wealth; that its absolute amount is a matter of indifference, because if every coin in existence were halved or doubled, it would discharge precisely the same function; and he inferred that the doctrine which tested the advantages of foreign commerce by the balance of trade or the net return of money, was altogether illusory. His theory is expounded in every elementary treatise on the subject. It may be urged that it was a mere truism, and therefore useless; or, again, that it does not enable us to deduce a complete theory of the functions of money. In regard to the first statement, I should reply that, although Smith probably misrepresented some of his antagonists, the fallacy which he exposed was not only current at the time, but is still constantly cropping up in modern controversies. So long as arguments are put forward which implicitly involve an erroneous, because self-contradictory, conception of the true functions of money, it is essential to keep in mind these first principles, however obvious they may be in an abstract statement. Euclid's axioms are useful because they are self-evident; and so long as people make mistakes in geometry, it will be necessary to expose their blundering by bringing out the contradictions involved. As Hobbes observed, people would dispute even geometrical axioms if they had an interest in doing so; and, certainly, they are ready to dispute the plainest doctrines about money. The other remark, that we cannot deduce a complete theory from the axiom is, of course, true. Thus, for example, although the doctrine may be unimpeachable, there is a difficulty in applying it to the facts. As gold has other uses besides its use as money, its value is not regulated exclusively by the principle assigned; as other things, again, such as bank-notes and cheques, discharge some of the functions of money, we have all manner of difficult problems as to what money precisely is, and how the most elementary principles will apply to the concrete facts. A very shrewd economist once remarked, listening to a metaphysical argument, " If there had been any money to be made out of it, we should have solved that question in the city long ago". Yet, there is surely money to be made out of a correct theory of the currency; and people in the city do not seem to have arrived at a complete agreement. In fact, such controversies illustrate the extreme difficulty which arises out of the complexity of the phenomena, even where the economic assumption of the action of purely money-loving activity is most nearly verified. The moral is, I fancy, that while inaccurate conclusions are extremely difficult, we can only hope to approach them by a firm grasp of the first principles revealed in the simplest cases.

Even in such a case, we have also to notice how we have to make allowance for the intrusion of other than purely economic cases. The doctrine just noticed is, of course, closely connected with the theory of free trade. The free trade argument is, I should mention, perfectly conclusive in a negative sense. It demonstrates, that is, the fallacy which lurks in the popular argument for protection. That argument belongs to the commonest class of economic fallacies, which consists in looking at one particular result without considering the necessary implications. The great advantage of any rational theory is, that it forces us to look upon the industrial mechanism as a whole, and to trace out the correlative changes involved in any particular operation. It disposes of the theories which virtually propose to improve our supply of water by pouring a cup out of one vessel into another; and such theories have had considerable success in economy. So far, in short, as a protectionist really maintains that the advantage consists in accumulating money, without asking what will be the effect upon the value of money, or that it consists in telling people to make for themselves what they could get on better terms by producing something to exchange for it, his arguments may be conclusively shown to be contradictory. Such arguments, at least, cannot be worth considering. But, to say nothing of cases which may be put by an ingenious disputant in which this may not quite apply, we have to consider reasons which may be extra-economical. When it is suggested, for example, that the economic disadvantage is a fair price for political independence; or, on the other hand, that the stimulus of competition is actually good for the trade affected; or, again, that protection tends naturally to corruption; we have arguments which, good or bad, are outside the sphere of economics proper. To answer them we have to enter the field of political or ethical inquiry, where we have to take leave of tangible facts and precise measures.

This is a more prominent element as we approach

the more human side (if I may so call it) of Political
Economy. Consider, for example, the doctrine which
made so profound an impression upon the old school
—Malthus's theory of population. It was summed
up in the famous—though admittedly inaccurate—
phrase, that population had a tendency to increase in
a geometrical ratio, while the means of subsistence
increased only in an arithmetical ratio. The food
available for each unit would therefore diminish
as the population increased. The so-called law
obviously states only a possibility. It describes a
"tendency," or, in other words, only describes what
would happen under certain, admittedly variable,
conditions. It showed how, in a limited area and
with the efficiency of industry remaining unaltered,
the necessary limits upon the numbers of the population would come into play. If, then, the law were
taken, or in so far as it was taken, to assert that, in
point of fact, the population must always be increas-
ing in civilised countries to the stage at which the
lowest class would be at starvation level, it was
certainly erroneous. There are cases in which
statesmen are alarmed by the failure of population to
show its old elasticity, and beginning to revert to the
view that an increased rate is desirable. It cannot
be said to be even necessarily true that in all cases
an increased population implies, of necessity, in-

creased difficulty of support. There are countries
which are inadequately peopled, and where greater
numbers would be able to support themselves more
efficiently because they could adopt a more elaborate organisation. Nor can it be said with certainty that some pressure may not, within limits,
be favourable to ultimate progress by stimulating the
energies of the people. In a purely stationary state
people might be too content with a certain stage of
comfort to develop their resources and attain a permanently higher stage. Whatever the importance
of such qualifications of the principle, there is a most
important conclusion to be drawn. Malthus or his
more rigid followers summed up their teaching by
one practical moral. The essential condition of
progress was, according to them, the discouragement
of early marriages. If, they held, people could only
be persuaded not to produce families until they had
an adequate prospect of supporting their families,
everything would go right. We shall not, I imagine,
be inclined to dispute the proposition, that a certain
degree of prudence and foresight is a quality of
enormous value; and that such a quality will manifest itself by greater caution in taking the most
important step in life. What such reasoners do not
appear to have appreciated was, the immense complexity and difficulty of the demand which they were

making. They seem to have fancied that it was possible simply to add another clause—the clause "Thou shalt not marry"—to the accepted code of morals ; and that, as soon as the evil consequences of the condemned behaviour were understood,—properly expounded, for example, in little manuals for the use of school children,—obedience to the new regulation would spontaneously follow. What they did not see, or did not fully appreciate, was the enormous series of other things—religious, moral, and intellectual—which are necessarily implied in altering the relation of the strongest human passion to the general constitution, and the impossibility of bringing home such an alteration, either by an act of legislation or by pointing out the bearing of a particular set of prudential considerations. Political Economy might be a very good thing; but its expositors were certainly too apt to think that it could by itself at once become a new gospel for mankind. Should we then infer from such criticisms that the doctrine of Malthus was false, or was of no importance ? Nothing would be further from my opinion. I hold, on the contrary, that it was of the highest importance, because it drew attention to a fact, the recognition of which was essential to all sound reasoning on social questions. The fact is, that population is not to be treated as a fixed quan-

tity, but as capable of rapid expansion; and that this
elasticity may at any moment require consideration,
and does in fact give the explanation of many important phenomena.   The main fact which gave
importance to Malthus's writings was the rapid and
enormous increase of pauperism during the first
quarter of this century. The charitable and senti-
mental writers of the day were alarmed, but proposed
to meet the evil by a reckless increase of charity,
either of the official or the private variety.   Pitt, we
know, declared (though he qualified the statement)
that to be the father of a large family should be a
source of honour, not of obloquy; and the measures
adopted under the influence of such notions did in
fact tend to diminish all sense of responsibility,
encouraged people to rely upon the parish for the
support of their children, and brought about a state
of things which alarmed all intelligent observers.
The greatest check to the evil was given by
the new Poor-law, adopted under the influence of
the principles advocated by Malthus and his friends.
His achievement, then, was not that he laid down
any absolutely correct scientific truth, or even said
anything which had not been more or less said by
many judicious people before his time; but that he
encouraged the application of a more systematic
method of reasoning upon the great problem of the

time.   Instead of simply giving way to the first
kindly impulse, abolishing a hardship here and distributing alms elsewhere, he substantially argued
that society formed a complex organism, whose
diseases should be considered physiologically, their
causes explained, and the appropriate remedies
considered in all their bearings.   We must not ask
simply whether we were giving a loaf to this or that
starving man, or indulge in *à priori* reasoning as to
the right of every human being to be supported by
others ; but treat the question as a physician should
treat a disease, and consider whether, on the whole,
the new regulations would increase or diminish the
causes of the existing evils.   He did not, therefore,
so much proclaim a new truth, as induce reformers
to place themselves at a new and a more rational
point of view.   The so-called law of population which
he announced might be in various ways inaccurate,
but the announcement made it necessary for rational
thinkers to take constantly into account considerations which are essential in any satisfactory
treatment of the great problems.   If it were right to
consider pauperism as a gulf of fixed dimensions, we
might hope to fill it by simply taking a sufficient
quantity of wealth from the richer classes.   If, as
Malthus urged, this process had a tendency to
enlarge the dimensions of the gulf itself, it was

obvious that the whole problem required a more elaborate treatment. By impressing people with this truth, and by showing how, in a great variety of cases, the elasticity of the population was a most important factor in determining the condition of the people, Malthus did a great service, and introduced a more systematic and scientific method of discussing the immensely important questions involved.

I will very briefly try to indicate one further application of economic principles. A critical point in the modern development of the study was marked by Mill's abandonment of the so-called "wage fund theory". That doctrine is now generally mentioned with contempt, as the most conspicuous instance of an entirely exploded theory. It is often said that it is either a falsity, or a barren truism. I am not about to argue the point, observing only that some very eminent Economists consider that it was rather inadequate than fallacious; and that to me it has always seemed that the theory which has really been confuted is not so much a theory which was ever actually held by Economists, as a formula into which they blundered when they tried to give a quasi-scientific definition of their meaning. It is common enough for people to argue sensibly, when the explicit statements of their argument may be altogether erroneous, At any rate, I think it has been a mis-

fortune that a good phrase has been discredited; and
that Mill's assailants, in exposing the errors of that
particular theory of a "wage fund," seemed to
imply that the whole conception of a "wage fund"
was a mistake.   For the result has been, that the
popular mind seems to regard the amount spent in
wages as an arbitrary quantity; as something which,
as Malthus put it, might be fixed at pleasure by her
Majesty's justices of the peace.   Because the law
was inaccurately stated, it is assumed that there is
no law at all, and that the share of the labourers in
the total product of industry might be fixed without
reference to the effect of a change upon the general
organisation.   Now, if the wage fund means the
share which, under existing circumstances, actually
goes to the class dependent upon wages, it is of
the highest importance to discover how that share
is actually determined; and it does not even follow
that a doctrine which is in some sense a truism
may not be a highly important doctrine.   One of the
ablest of the old Economists, Nassan Senior, after
laying down his version of the theory, observes
that it is "so nearly self-evident" that if Political
Economy were a new science, it might be taken
for granted.   But he proceeds to enumerate seven
different opinions, some of them held by many people,
and others by writers of authority, with which it is

inconsistent. And, without following his arguments, this statement suggests what I take to be a really relevant defence of his reasons. At the time when the theory was first formulated, there were many current doctrines which were self-contradictory, and which could, therefore, best be met by the assertion of a truism. When the peace of 1815 brought distress instead of plenty, some people, such as Southey, thought it a sufficient explanation to say that the manufacturer had lost his best customer, because the Government wanted fewer guns and less powder. They chose to overlook the obvious fact that a customer who pays for his goods by taking money out of the pockets of the seller, is not an unmixed blessing. Then, there was the theory of general "gluts," and of what is still denounced as over-production. The best cure for commercial distress would be, as one disputant asserted, to burn all the goods in our warehouses. It was necessary to point out that this theory (when stated in superficial terms) regarded superabundance of wealth as the cause of universal poverty. Another common theory was the evil effect of manufacturers in displacing work. The excellent Robert Owen stated it as an appalling fact, that the cotton manufacture supplanted the labour of a hundred (perhaps it was two hundred) millions of men. He seems to assume that, if the machinery had not been there, there would still have been wages for the hundred millions. The curious confusion, indeed, which leads us to speak of men wanting work, when what we really mean is that they want wages, shows the tenacity of an old fallacy. Mandeville argued long ago that the fire of London was a blessing, because it set at work so many carpenters, plumbers, and glaziers. The Protestant Reformation had done less good than the invention of hooped petticoats, which had provided employment for so many milliners. I shall not insult you by exposing fallacies; and yet, so long as they survive, they have to be met by truisms. While people are proposing to lengthen their blankets by cutting off one end to sew upon the other, one has to point out that the total length remains constant. Now, I fancy that, in point of fact, these fallacies are often to be found in modern times. I read, the other day, in the papers, an argument, adduced by some advocate, on behalf of the Eight Hours Bill. He wished, he said, to make labour dear, and would therefore make it scarce. This apparently leads to the conclusion that the less people work the more they will get, which I take to be a fallacy. So, to mention nothing else, it is still apparently a common argument in favour of protection in America, that the native labourer requires to be supported against the pauperised labour of Europe. Americans in general are to be made richer by paying higher prices, and by being forced to produce commodities which they could get with less labour employed on the production of other things in exchange. I will not go further; for I think that no one who reads the common arguments can be in want of sufficient illustrations of popular fallacies. This, I say, is some justification for dwelling upon the contrary truisms. I admit, indeed, that even these fallacies may apply to particular cases in which they may represent partial truths; and I also agree that, as sometimes stated, the wage fund theory was not only a truism, but a fruitless truism. It was, however, as I believe, an attempt to generalise a very pertinent and important doctrine, as to the way in which the actual competition in which labourers and employers are involved, actually operates. If so, it requires rather modification than indiscriminate denunciation; and it is, I believe, so treated by the best modern Economists.

I consider, then, that the Economists were virtually attempting to describe systematically the main relations of the industrial mechanism. They showed what were the main functions which it, in fact, discharges. Their theory was sufficient to expose many errors, especially those which arise from looking solely at one part of a complex process, and neglecting the implied reactions. It enabled them to point out the inconsistencies and actual contradictions involved in many popular arguments, which are still very far from being destroyed. Their main error—apart from any particular logical slips—was, namely, that when they had laid down certain principles which belong properly to the prolegomena of the science, and which are very useful when regarded as providing logical tests of valid reasoning, they imagined that they had done a great deal more, and that the desired science was actually constituted. They laid down three or four primary axioms, such as the doctrine that men desire wealth, and fancied that the whole theory could be deduced from them. This, if what I have said be true, was really to misunderstand what they were really doing. It was to suppose that you could obtain a description of social phenomena without examining the actual structure of society; and was as erroneous as to suppose that you could deduce physiological truths from a few general propositions about the mechanical relations of the skeleton. Such criticisms have been made by the historical school of Economists; and I, at least, can fully accept their general view. I quite agree that the old assumptions of the older school were frequently unjustifiable ; nor can I deny that they laid them down with a tone of superlative dogmatism, which was apt to be very offensive, and which was not justified by their position. Moreover, I entirely agree that the progress of economic science, and of all other moral sciences, requires a historical basis; and that we should make a very great blunder if we thought that the creation of an economic man would justify us in dispensing with an investigation of concrete facts, both of the present day and of earlier stages of industrial evolution. But to this there is an obvious qualification. What do we mean by investigating facts? It seems to be a very simple rule, but it leads us at once to great difficulties. So, as Mill and later writers have very rightly asked, how are we to settle even the most obvious questions in inquiries where, for obvious reasons, we cannot make experiments, and where we have not such a set of facts as would spontaneously give us the truths which we might seek by experiment? Take, as Mill suggested, such a question as free trade. We cannot get two countries alike in all else, and differing only in respect to their adoption or rejection of a protective tariff. Anything like a thoroughgoing system of free trade has been tried in England alone; and the commercial prosperity of the country since its adoption has been affected by innumerable conditions, so that it is altogether impossible to isolate the results which are to be attributed to the negative condition of the absence of protection. Briefly, the result is that the phenomena with which we have to deal are so complex, and our power of arranging them so as to unravel the complexity is so limited, that the direct method of observation breaks down altogether. Mill confessed the necessity of applying a different method, which he described with great ability, and which substantially amounts to the method of the older Economists. If, with some writers of the historical school, we admit the objections which apply to this method, we seem to be reduced to a hopeless state of uncertainty. A treatise on Political Economy becomes nothing but a miscellaneous collection of facts, with no definite clue or uniform method of reasoning. I must beg, in conclusion, to indicate what, so far as I can guess, seems to be the view suggested in presence of this difficulty.

If I am asked whether Political Economy, understood, for example, as Mill understood it, is to be regarded as a science, I should have to admit that I could not simply reply, Yes. To say nothing of any errors in his logic, I should say that I do not believe that it gives us sufficient guidance even in regard to economic phenomena. We could not, that is, deduce from the laws accepted by Economists the necessary working of any given measure—say, the effect of protection or free trade, or, still more, the making of a

poor-law system.   Such problems involve elements
of which the Economist, purely as an Economist, is an
incompetent judge; and the further we get from
those questions in which purely economical considerations are dominant, towards those in which
other factors become relevant,—from questions as to
currency, for example, to questions as to the relations of capitalists and labourers,—the greater the
inadequacy of our methods.   But I also hold that
Political Economists may rightly claim a certain
scientific character for their speculations.   If their
ultimate aim is to frame a science of economics
which shall be part of the science—not yet constituted—of sociology, then I should say that
what they have really done—so far as they have
reasoned accurately—has been to frame an essential part of the prolegomena to such a science.
The "laws" which they have tried to formulate
are not laws which, even if established, would enable
us to predict the results of any given action; but
they are laws which would have to be taken into
account in attempting any such prediction.   And
this is so, I think, because the laws are descriptions
—within limits accurate descriptions—of actually
existing facts as to the social mechanism.   They are
not mere abstract hypotheses, in the sense sometimes
attached to that phrase; but accounts of the plan

upon which the industrial arrangements of civilised
countries are, as a matter of fact, constructed. Such
a classification and systematic account of facts is, as
I should suggest, absolutely necessary for any sound
historical method.   Facts are not simply things
lying about, which anybody can pick up and describe
for the mere pains of collecting them.   We cannot
even see a fact without reflection and observation and
judgment; and to arrange them in an order which
shall be both systematic and fruitful, to look at them
from that point of view in which we can detect
the general underlying principles, is, in all cases, an
essential process before we can begin to apply a truly
historical method.   Anything, it is said, may be
proved by facts; and that is painfully true until we
have the right method of what has been called
"colligating" facts.   The Catholic and the Protestant, the Conservative and the Radical, the
Individualist and the Socialist, have equal facility in
proving their own doctrines with arguments, which
habitually begin, "All history shows".   Printers
should be instructed always to strike out that phrase
as an erratum; and to substitute, "I choose to take
for granted".   In order to judge between them we
have to come to some conclusion as to what is the
right method of conceiving of history, and probably
to try many methods before reaching that which

arranges the shifting and complicated chaos of phenomena in something like an intelligible order. A first step and a necessary basis, as I believe, for all the more complex inquiries will have to be found by disentangling the various orders of laws (if I may so speak), and considering by themselves those laws of industrial growth which are nearest to the physical sciences in certain respects, and which, within certain limits, can be considered apart, inasmuch as they represent the working of forces which are comparatively independent of forces of a higher order. What I should say for Political Economists is that they have done a good deal in this direction; that they have explained, and, I suppose, with considerable accuracy, what is the actual nature of the industrial mechanism; that they have explained fairly its working in certain cases where the economic are practically also the sole or dominant motives; and that they have thus laid down certain truths which require attention even when we take into account the play of other more complex and, as we generally say, higher motives. We may indeed hope and believe that society will ultimately be constituted upon a different system; and that for the organisation which has spontaneously and unconsciously developed itself, another will be substituted which will correspond more closely to some principles of justice, and give freer scope for the full development of the human faculties. That is a very large question: I only say that, in any case, all genuine progress consists in a development of institutions already existing, and therefore that a full understanding of the working of the present system is essential to a rational consideration of possible improvements. The Socialist may look forward to a time—let us hope that it may come soon!—when nobody will have any grievances. But his schemes will be the better adapted for the realisation of his hopes in proportion as he has fully understood what is the part played by each factor of the existing system; what is its function, and how that function may be more efficiently discharged by any substitute. Only upon that condition can he avoid the common error of inventing some scheme which is in sociology what schemes for perpetual motion are in mechanics; plans for making everything go right by condemning some existing portion of the system without fully understanding how it has come into existence, and what is the part which it plays in the whole. I think myself that a study of the good old orthodox system of Political Economy is useful in this sense, even where it is wrong; because at least it does give a system, and therefore forces its opponents to present an alternative system, instead of simply cutting a hole in the shoe when it pinches, or striking out the driving wheel because it happens to creak unpleasantly.   And I think so the more because I cannot but observe that whenever a real economic question presents itself, it has to be argued on pretty much the old principles, unless we take the heroic method of discarding argument altogether.   I should be the last to deny that the old Political Economy requires careful revision and modification, and equally slow to deny that the limits of its applicability require to be carefully defined.   But, with these qualifications, I say, with equal conviction, that it does lay down principles which require study and consideration, for the simple reason that they assert the existence of facts which are relevant and important in all the most vitally interesting problems of to-day.

THE MORALITY OF COMPETITION.

WHEN it has occurred to me to say—as I have occasionally said—that, to my mind, the whole truth
lies neither with the individualist nor with his
antagonist, my friends have often assured me that I
was illogical. Of two contradictory principles, they
say, you must take one. There are cases, I admit,
in which this remark applies. It is true, or it is not
true, that two and two make four. We cannot, in
arithmetic, adopt Sir Roger de Coverley's concilia-
tory view, that there is much to be said on both
sides. But this logical rule supposes that, in point
of fact, the two principles apply to the same case, and
are mutually exclusive. I also think that the habit
of taking for granted that social problems are re-
ducible to such an alternative, is the source of innumerable fallacies. I hold that, as a rule, any
absolute solution of such problems is impossible; and
that a man who boasts of being logical, is generally
announcing his deliberate intention to be one-sided.
He is confusing the undeniable canon that of two
contradictory propositions one must be true, with the

assumption that two propositions are really contradictory. The apparent contradiction may be illusory.
Society, says the individualist, is made up of all
its members.   Certainly: if all Englishmen died,
there would be no English race.   But it does not
follow that every individual Englishman is not also
the product of the race.   Society, says the Socialist,
is an organic whole.   I quite admit the fact; but it
does not follow that, as a whole, it has any qualities
or aims independent of the qualities and aims of the
constituent parts.   Metaphysicians have amused
themselves, in all ages, with the puzzle about the
many and the one.   Perhaps they may find contradictions in the statement that a human society is both
one and many; a unit and yet complex; but I am
content to assume that unless we admit the fact, we
shall get a very little way in sociology.

Society, we say, is an organism.   That implies
that every part of a society is dependent upon the
other parts, and that although, for purposes of argument, we may find it convenient to assume that
certain elements remain fixed while others vary, we
must always remember that this is an assumption
which, in the long run, never precisely corresponds
to the facts.   We may, for example, in economical
questions, attend simply to the play of the ordinary
industrial machinery, without taking into account

the fact that the industrial machinery is conditioned by the political and ecclesiastical constitution, by the whole social order, and, therefore, by the acceptance of corresponding ethical, or philosophical or scientific creeds. The method is justifiable so long as we remember that we are using a logical artifice; but we blunder if we take our hypothesis for a full statement of the actual facts. We are then tempted, and it is, perhaps, the commonest of all sources of error in such inquiries, to assume that conditions are absolute which are really contingent; or, to attend only to the action, without noticing the inevitable reactions of the whole system of institutions. And I would suggest, that from this follows a very important lesson in such inquiries. To say that this or that part of a system is bad, is to say, by implication, that some better arrangement is possible consistently with our primary assumptions. In other words, we cannot rationally propose simply to cut out one part of a machine, dead or living, without considering the effect of the omission upon all the other dependent parts. The whole system is necessarily altered. What, we must therefore ask, is the tacit implication as well as what is the immediate purpose of a change? May not the bad effect be a necessary part of the system to which we also owe the good; or necessary under some conditions? It is always,

therefore, a relevant question, what is the suggested
alternative? We can then judge whether the re-
moval of a particular evil is or is not to be produced
at a greater cost than it is worth; whether it would
be a process, say, of really curing a smoky chimney
or of stopping the chimney altogether, and so abolishing not only the smoke but the fire.

I propose to apply this to the question of "competition". Competition is frequently denounced as
the source of social evils. The complaint is far from
a new one. I might take for my text a passage from
J. S. Mill's famous chapter on the probable future of
the labouring classes. Mill, after saying that he
agrees with the Socialists in their practical aims,
declares his utter dissent from their declamations
against competition. "They forget," he says, "that
where competition is not, monopoly is; and that
monopoly, in all its forms, is the taxation of the
industrious for the support of indolence, if not of
plunder." That suggests my question: If competition is bad, what is good? What is the alternative
to competition? Is it, as Mill says, monopoly, or is
any third choice possible? If it is monopoly, do you
defend monopoly, or only monopoly in some special
cases? I opened, not long ago, an old book of carica-
tures, in which the revolutionary leader is carrying a
banner with the double inscription, "No monopoly!

No competition!" The implied challenge—how can
you abolish both ?—seemed to me to require a plain
answer.   Directly afterwards I then took up the
newspaper, and read the report of an address upon
the prize-day of a school.   The speaker dwelt in the
usual terms upon the remorseless and crushing competition of the present day, which he mentioned as
an incitement to every boy to get a good training for
the struggle.   The moral was excellent; but it
seemed to me curious that the speaker should be
denouncing competition in the very same breath
with proofs of its influence in encouraging education.
When I was a lad, a clever boy and a stupid boy had
an equal chance of getting an appointment to a
public office.   The merit which won a place might
be relationship to a public official, or perhaps to a
gentleman who had an influence in the constituency
of the official.   The system was a partial survival of
the good old days in which, according to Sam
Weller, the young nobleman got a position because
his mother's uncle's wife's grandfather had once
lighted the King's pipe.   The nobleman, I need
hardly add, considered this as an illustration of the
pleasant belief, "Whatever is, is right".   As we had
ceased to accept that opinion in politics, offices were
soon afterwards thrown open to competition, with
the general impression that we were doing justice

and opening a career to merit. That the resulting system has grave defects is, I think, quite undeniable; but so far as it has succeeded in determining that the men should be selected for public duty, for their fitness, and for nothing else, it is surely a step in advance which no one would now propose to retrace. And yet it was simply a substitution of competition for monopoly. As it comes into wider operation, some of us begin to cry out against competition. The respectable citizen asks, What are we to do with our boys? The obvious reply is, that he really means, What are we to do with our fools? A clever lad can now get on by his cleverness; and of course those who are not clever are thrust aside. That is a misfortune, perhaps, for them; but we can hardly regard it as a misfortune for the country. And clearly, too, pressure of this kind is likely to increase. We have come to believe that it is a main duty of the nation to provide general education. When the excellent Miss Hannah More began to spread village schools, she protested warmly that she would not teach children anything which would tend to make the poor discontented with their station. They must learn to read the Bible, but she hoped that they would stop short of such knowledge as would enable them to read Tom Paine. Now, Hannah More deserves our gratitude for her share in setting the ball rolling; but it has rolled far beyond the limits she would have prescribed. We now desire not only that every child in the country should be able to acquire the elements of learning at least; but, further, we hope that ladders may be provided by which every promising child may be able to climb beyond the elements, and to acquire the fullest culture of which his faculties are capable. There is not only no credit at the present day in wishing so much, but it is discreditable not to do what lies in one's power to further its accomplishment. But, then, is not that to increase enormously the field of competition? I, for example, am a literary person, after a fashion; I have, that is, done something to earn a living by my pen. I had the advantage at starting of belonging to the small class which was well enough off to send its children to the best schools and universities. That is to say, I was one of the minority which had virtually a monopoly of education, and but for that circumstance I should in all probability have taken to some possibly more honest, but perhaps even worse paid, occupation. Every extension of the margin of education, everything which diffuses knowledge and intellectual training through a wider circle, must increase the competition among authors. If every man with brains, whether born in a palace or a cottage is to have a chance of making the best of them, the capacity for authorship, and therefore the number of competitors, will be enormously spread. It may also, we will hope, increase the demand for their work. The same remark applies to every profession for which intellectual culture is a qualification. Do we regret the fact? Would we sentence three-quarters of the nation to remain stupid, in order that the fools in the remaining quarter may have a better chance? That would be contrary to every democratic instinct, to the highest as well as the lowest. But if I say, every office and every profession shall be open to every man; success in it shall depend upon his abilities and merits; and, further, every child in the country shall have the opportunity of acquiring the necessary qualifications, what is that but to accept and to stimulate the spirit of competition? What, I ask, is the alternative? Should people be appointed by interest? Or is nobody to be anxious for official or professional or literary or commercial success, but only to develop his powers from a sense of duty, and wait till some infallible observer comes round and says, "Friend, take this position, which you deserve"? Somehow I do not think that last scheme practicable at present. But, even in that case, I do not see how the merits of any man are to be tested without enabling him to prove by experiment that he is the most meritorious person ; and, if that be admitted, is not every step in promoting education, in equalising, therefore, the position from which men start for the race, a direct encouragement to competition ?

Carlyle was fond of saying that Napoleon's great message to mankind was the declaration that careers should be open to talent, or the tools given to him who could use them.   Surely that was a sound principle ; and one which, so far as I can see, cannot be applied without stimulating competition.   The doctrine, indeed, is unpalatable to many Socialists. To me, it seems to be one to which only the cowardly and the indolent can object in principle.   Will not a society be the better off, in which every man is set to work upon the tasks for which he is most fitted ?   If we allowed our teaching and our thinking to be done by blockheads; our hard labour to be done by men whose muscles were less developed than their brains ; made our soldiers out of our cowards, and our sailors out of the sea-sick,—should we be better off?   It seems, certainly, to me, that whatever may be the best constitution of society, one mark of it will be the tendency to distribute all social functions according to the fitness of the agents ; to place trust where trust is, justifiable, and to give the fullest scope for every proved ability, intellectual, moral, and physical.

Of course, such approximation to this result, as we can observe in the present order of things, is very imperfect. Many of the most obvious evils in the particular system of competition now adopted, may be summed up in the statement, that the tests according to which success is awarded, are not so contrived as to secure the success of the best competitors. Some of them, for example, are calculated to give an advantage to the superficial and the showy. But that is to say that they are incompatible with the true principle which they were intended to embody; and that we should reform our method, not in the direction of limiting competition, but in the direction of so framing our system that it may be a genuine application of Carlyle's doctrine. In other words, in all the professions for which intellectual excellence is required, the conditions should be such as to give the best man the best chance, as far as human arrangements can secure that object. What other rule can be suggested? Competition, in this sense, means the preservation of the very atmosphere which is necessary to health; and to denounce it is either to confirm the most selfish and retrograde principles, or to denounce something which is only called competition by a confusion of ideas. How easy such a confusion may be, is obvious when we look at the ordinary language about industrial competition. We are told that wages are kept down by competition. To this Mill replied in the passage I have quoted, and, upon his own theory, at any rate, replied with perfect justice, that they were also kept up by competition. The common language upon the subject is merely one instance of the fallacies into which men fall when they personify an abstraction. Competition becomes a kind of malevolent and supernatural being, to whose powers no conceivable limits are assigned. It is supposed to account for any amount of degradation. Yet if, by multiplying their numbers, workmen increase supply, and so lower the price of labour, it follows, conversely, by the very same reasoning, that if they refused to multiply, they would diminish the supply and raise the price. The force, by its very nature, operates as certainly in one direction as in the other. If, again, there is competition among workmen, there is competition among capitalists. In every strike, of course, workmen apply the principle, and sometimes apply it very effectually, in the attempt to raise their wages. It was often argued, indeed, that in this struggle, the employer possessed advantages partly due to his power of forming tacit combinations. The farmers in a parish, or the manufacturers in a business, were pledged to each other not to raise the rate of wages. If that be so, you again complain, not of competition,

but of the want of competition; and you agree that
the labourer will benefit, as in fact, I take it, he has
undoubtedly benefited, by freer competition among
capitalists, or by the greater power of removing his
own labour to better markets. In such cases, the
very meaning of the complaint is not that there is
competition, but that the competition is so arranged
as to give an unfair advantage to one side. And a
similar misunderstanding is obviously implied in
other cases. The Australian or American workman
fears that his wages will be lowered by the competition of the Chinese; and the Englishman protests
against the competition of pauper aliens. Let us
assume that he is right in believing that such competition will tend to lower his wages, whatever the
moral to be drawn from the fact. Briefly, denunciations of "competition" in this sense are really
complaints that we do not exclude the Chinese immi-
grant and therefore give a monopoly to the native
labourer. That may be a good thing for him, and if
it be not a good thing for the Chinaman who is excluded from the field, we perhaps do not care very
much about the results to China. We are so much
better than the heathen that we need not bother
about their interests. But, of course, the English
workman, when he complains of the intensity of
competition, does not propose to adopt the analogous

remedy of giving a monopoly to one section of our own population. The English pauper is here; we do not want to suppress him, but only to suppress his pauperism; and he certainly cannot be excluded from any share in the fund devoted to the support of labour. The evil, therefore, of which we complain is primarily the inadequacy of the support provided, not,—though that may also be complained of,—the undesirable method by which those funds are distributed. In other words, the complaint may so far be taken to mean that there are too many competitors, not that, given the competitors, their shares are determined by competition, instead of being determined by monopoly or by some other principle.

We have therefore to inquire whether any principle can be suggested which will effect the desired end, and which will yet really exclude competition. The popular suggestion is that the remedy lies in suppressing competition by equalising the prizes. If no prizes are to be won, there will so far be less reason for competing. Enough may be provided for all by simply taking something from those who have too much. Now, I may probably assume that we all agree in approving the contemplated end—a greater equality of wealth, and especially an elevation of the lower classes to a higher position in

the scale of comfort. Every social reformer, whatever his particular creed, would probably agree that
some of us are too rich, and that a great many are
too poor.   But we still have to ask, in what sense it
is conceivable that a real suppression of competition
can contribute to the desired end.   It is obvious that
when we denounce competition we often mean not
that it is to be abolished, but that it is to be
regulated and limited in its application.   So, for
example, people sometimes speak as if competition
were the antithesis to co-operation.   But I need
hardly say that individualists, as well as their
opponents, may legitimately sing the praises of co-
operation. Nobody was more forward than Mill, for
example, and Mill's followers, in advocating the
principles of the early co-operative societies.   He
and they rejoiced to believe that the co-operative societies had revealed unsuspected virtues and
capacities in the class from which they sprang; that
they had done much to raise the standard of life
and to extend sympathy and human relations among
previously disconnected units of society. But it is, of
course, equally obvious that they have grown up in a
society which supposes free competition in every part
of its industrial system; that co-operative societies,
so far as the outside world is concerned, have to buy
in the cheapest and sell in the dearest market; that

the rate of wages of their members is still fixed by competition; and that they encourage habits of saving and forethought which presuppose that each man is to have private ends of his own. In what sense, then, can co-operation ever be regarded as really opposed to competition? Competition may exist among groups of men just as much as among individuals: a state of war is not less a state of war if it is carried on by regiments and armies, instead of by mere chaotic struggles in which each man fights for his own hand. Competition does not mean that there should be no combination, but that there should be no monopoly. So long as a trade or a profession is open to every one who chooses to take it up, its conduct will be equally regulated by competition, whether it be competition as between societies or individuals, or whether its profits be divided upon one system or another between the various classes concerned. Co-operators, of course, may look forward to a day in which society at large will be members of a single co-operative society; or, again, to a time in which every industrial enterprise may be conducted by the State. Supposing any such aspiration to be realised, the question still remains, whether they would amount to the abolition or still only to the shifting of the incidence of competition. Socialists tell us that hitherto the labourer has not had his fair share of the produce of industry. The existing system has sanctioned a complicated chicanery, by which one class has been enabled to live as mere bloodsuckers and parasites upon the rest of society. Property is the result of theft, instead of being, as Economists used to assure us, the reward of thrift. It is hoped that these evils may be remedied by a reconstruction of society, in which the means of production shall all be public property, and every man's income be simply a salary in proportion to the quantity of his labour. If we, then, ask how far competition would be abolished, we may first make one remark. Such a system, like every other system, requires, for its successful working, that the instincts and moral impulses should correspond to the demands of the society. Absolute equality of property is just as compatible with universal misery as with universal prosperity. A population made up of thoroughly lazy, sensual, stupid individuals could, if it chose, work such a machinery so as to suppress all who were industrious, refined and intelligent. However great may be the revenue of a nation, it is a very simple problem of arithmetic to discover how many people could be supported just above the starvation level. The nation at large would, on the supposed system, have to decide how its numbers and wants are to be proportioned to its means. If individuals do not compete, the whole society has, presumably, to compete with other societies; and, in every case whatever, with the general forces of nature. An indolent and inefficient majority might decide, if it pleased, that the amount of work to be exacted should be that which would be just enough to provide the simplest material necessities. If, again, the indolent and inefficient are to exist at all,—and we can scarcely count upon their disappearance,—and if further, they are to share equally with the industrious and the efficient, we must, in some way, coerce them into the required activity. If every industrial organisation is to be worked by the State, the State, it would seem, must appeal to the only means at its disposal,—namely, the prison and the scourge. If, moreover, the idle and sensual choose to multiply, the State must force them to refrain, or the standard of existence will be lowered. And, therefore, as is often argued, Socialism logically carried out would, under such conditions, lead to slavery; to a state in which labour would be enforced, and the whole system of life absolutely regulated by the will of the majority; and, in the last resort, by physical force. That seems, I confess, to be a necessary result, unless you can assume a moral change, which is entirely different from the mere change of

machinery, and not necessarily implied, nor even
made probable, by the change. The intellectual
leaders of Socialism, no doubt, assume that the re-
moval of " injustice " will lead to the development of
a public spirit which will cause the total efficiency to
be as great as it is at present, or perhaps greater.
But the mass who call themselves Socialists take,
one suspects, a much simpler view. They are
moved by the very natural, but not especially lofty,
desire to have more wages and less work. They
take for granted that if their share of the total product is increased, they will get a larger dividend;
and do not stop to inquire whether the advantage
may be not more than counterbalanced by the
diminution of the whole product, when the present
incitements to industry are removed. They argue,
—that is, so far as they argue at all,—as though the
quantity to be distributed were a fixed quantity, and
regard capitalists as pernicious persons, somehow
intercepting a lion's share of the stream of wealth
which, it is assumed, would flow equally if they were
abolished. That is, of course, to beg the whole
question.

I, however, shall venture to assume that the industrial machinery requires a corresponding moral
force to work it; and I, therefore, proceed to ask
how such a force can be supposed to act without

some form of competition.   Nothing, as a recent writer suggests,—ironically, perhaps,—could be easier than to secure an abolition of competition.   You have only to do two things: to draw a "ring-fence" round your society, and then to proportion the members within the fence to the supplies.   The remark suggests the difficulty.   A ring-fence, for example, round London or Manchester would mean the starvation of millions in a month ; or, if round England, the ruin of English commerce, the enormous rise in the cost of the poor man's food, and the abolition of all his little luxuries.   But, if you include even a population as large as London, what you have next to do is to drill some millions of people—vast numbers of them poor, reckless, ignorant, sensual, and selfish—to regulate their whole mode of life by a given code, and refrain from all the pleasures which they most·appreciate.   The task is a big one, and not the less if you have also to undertake that everybody, whatever his personal qualities, shall have enough to lead a comfortable life.   I do not suppose, however, that any rational Socialist would accept that programme of isolation.   He would hold that, in his Utopia, we can do more efficiently all that is done under a system which he regards as wasteful and unjust.   The existing machinery, whatever else may be said of it, does, in fact, tend to weld the

whole world more and more into a single industrial
organism. English workmen are labouring to satisfy
the wants of other human beings in every quarter of
the world ; while Chinese, and Africans, and Europeans, and Americans are also labouring to satisfy
theirs. This vast and almost inconceivably complex
machinery has grown up in the main unconsciously,
or, at least, with a very imperfect anticipation of
the ultimate results, by the independent efforts
of innumerable inventors, and speculators, and
merchants, and manufacturers, each of them
intent, as a rule, only upon his own immediate
profits and the interests of the little circle with which
he is in immediate contact. The theory is not, I
suppose, that this gigantic system of mutual inter-
dependence should be abolished or restricted, but
that it should be carried on consciously, with definite
and intelligible purpose, and in such a way as to
promote the interests of every fraction of society.
The whole organism should resemble one worked by
a single brain, instead of representing the resultant
of a multitude of distracted and conflicting forces.
The difficulties are obvious enough, nor need I dwell
upon them here. I will not inquire whether it does
not suppose something like omniscience in the new
industrial leaders ; and whether the restless and
multifarious energy now displayed in discovering

new means of satisfying human wants could be supplied by a central body, or a number of central bodies, made up of human beings, and, moreover, official human beings, reluctant to try experiments and strike into new courses, and without the present motives for enterprise. "Individualists" have enlarged sufficiently upon such topics. What I have to note is that, in any case, the change supposes the necessity of a corresponding morality in the growth of the instincts, the public spirit, the hatred of indolence, the temperance and self-command which would be requisite to work it efficiently. The organisation into which we are born presupposes certain moral instincts, and, moreover, necessarily implies a vast system of moral discipline. Our hopes and aspirations, our judgments of our neighbours and of ourselves, are at every moment guided and moulded by the great structure of which we form a part. Whenever we ask how our lives are to be directed, what are to be the terms on which we form our most intimate ties, whom we are to support or suppress, how we are to win respect or incur contempt, we are profoundly affected by the social relations in which we are placed at our birth, and the corresponding beliefs or prejudices which we have unconsciously imbibed. Such influences, it may perhaps be said, are of incomparably greater importance than the direct exhortations to which we listen, or than the abstract doctrines which we accept in words, but which receive their whole colouring from the concrete facts to which they conform. Now, I ask how such discipline can be conceived without some kind of competition; or, rather, what would be the discipline which would remain if, in some sense, competition could be suppressed? If in the ideal society there are still prizes to be won, positions which may be the object of legitimate desire, and if those positions are to be open to every one, whatever his circumstances, we might still have the keenest competition, though carried on by different methods. If, on the other hand, no man's position were to be better than another's, we might suppress competition at the price of suppressing every motive for social as well as individual improvement. In any conceivable state of things, the welfare of every society, the total means of enjoyment at its disposal, must depend upon the energy, intelligence, and trustworthiness of its constituent members. Such qualities, I need hardly say, are qualities of individuals. Unless John and Peter and Thomas are steady, industrious, sober, and honest, the society as a whole will be neither honest nor sober nor prosperous. The problem, then, becomes, how can you ensure the existence of such qualities unless John and Peter and the rest have some advantage in virtue of possessing them ? Somehow or other, a man must be the better off for doing his work well and treating his neighbour fairly. He ought surely to hold the positions in which such qualities are most required, and to have, if possible, the best chance of being a progenitor of the rising generation. A social condition in which it made no difference to a man, except so far as his own conscience was concerned, whether he were or were not honest, would imply a society favourable to people without a conscience, because giving full play to the forces which make for corruption and disintegration. If you remove the rewards accessible to the virtuous and peaceful, how are you to keep the penalties which restrain the vicious and improvident ? A bare repeal of the law, " If a man will not work, neither shall he eat," would not of itself promote industry. You would at most remove the compulsion which arises from competition, to introduce the compulsion which uses physical force. You would get rid of what seems to some people the " natural " penalty of want following waste, and be forced to introduce the "arti-ficial " or legislative penalty of compulsory labour. But, otherwise, you must construct your society so that, by the spontaneous play of society, the purer elements may rise to the surface, and the scum sink to the bottom. So long as human nature varies

indefinitely, so long as we have knaves and honest
men, sinners and saints, cowards and heroes, some
process of energetic and active sifting is surely
essential to the preservation of social health; and it
is difficult to see how that is conceivable without
some process of active and keen competition.

The Socialist will, of course, say, and say with too
much truth, that the present form of competition is
favourable to anti-social qualities.   If, indeed, a
capitalist is not a person who increases the productive powers of industry, but a person who
manages simply to intercept a share produced by the
industry of others, there is, of course, much to be said
for this view.   I cannot now consider that point, for
my subject to-day is the moral aspect of competition
considered generally.   And what I have just said
suggests what is, I think, the more purely moral
aspect of the question.   A reasonable Socialist
desires to maintain what is good in the existing
system, while suppressing its abuses.   The question,
What is good? is partly economical; but it is partly
also ethical: and it is with that part that I am at
present concerned.

Any system of competition, any system which
supposes a reward for virtue other than virtue itself,
may be accused of promoting selfishness and other
ugly qualities.   The doctrine that virtue is its own

reward is very charming in the mouth of the virtuous man; but when his neighbours use it as an excuse for not rewarding him, it becomes rather less attractive.   It saves a great deal of trouble, no doubt, and relieves us from an awkward responsibility.   I must, however, point out, in the first place, that a fallacy is often introduced into these discussions which Mr. Herbert Spencer has done a great deal to expose.   He has dwelt very forcibly, for example, on the fact that it is a duty to be happy and healthy; and that selfishness, if used in a bad sense, should not mean simply regard for ourselves, but only disregard for our neighbours.   We ought not, in other words, to be unjust because we ourselves happen to be the objects of injustice.   The parable of the good Samaritan is generally regarded as a perfect embodiment of a great moral truth.   Translated from poetry into an abstract logical form, it amounts to saying that we should do good to the man who most needs our services, whatever be the accidents which alienate ordinary sympathies.   Now, suppose that the good Samaritan had himself fallen among thieves, what would have been his duty? His first duty, I should say, would have been, if possible, to knock down the thief; his second, to tie up his own wounds; and his third, to call in the police.   We should not, perhaps, call him virtuous for

such conduct; but we should clearly think him
wrong for omitting it.   Not to resist a thief is
cowardly; not to attend to your own health is to
incapacitate yourself for duty: not to apply to the
police is to be wanting in public spirit.   Assuming
robbery to be wrong, I am not the less bound to
suppress it because I happen to be the person
robbed; I am only bound not to be vindictive—that
is, not to allow my personal feelings to make me act
otherwise than I should act if I had no special
interest in the particular case.   Adam Smith's
favourite rule of the "indifferent spectator" is the
proper one in the case.   I should be impartial, and
incline no more to severity than to lenity, because I
am forced by circumstances to act both as judge and
as plaintiff.   So, in questions of self-support, it is
obviously a fallacy to assume that an action, directed
in the first instance to a man's own benefit, is therefore to be stigmatised as selfish.   On the good
Samaritan's principle, a person should be supported,
ceteris paribus, by the person who can do it most
efficiently, and in nine cases out of ten that person is
himself.   If self-support is selfish in the sense that
the service is directly rendered to self, it is not the
less unselfish in so far as it is necessarily also a
service to others.   If I keep myself by my labour, I
am preventing a burden from falling upon my

fellows.   And, of course, the case is stronger when I
include my family.   We were all impressed the other
day by the story of the poor boy who got some
wretchedly small pittance by his work, spent a small
portion of it upon his own needs, and devoted the
chief part of it to trying to save his mother and her
other children from starvation.   Was he selfish?
Was he selfish even in taking something for himself,
as the only prop of his family?   What may be the
immediate motive of a man when he is working for
his own bread and the bread of his family may often
be a difficult question; but as, in point of fact, he is
helping not only himself and those who depend on
him, but also in some degree relieving others from a
burden, his conduct must clearly not be set down
as selfish in any sense which involves moral dis-
approval.

Let us apply this to the case of competition.   The
word is generally used to convey a suggestion of
selfishness in a bad sense.   We think of the hardship
upon the man who is ousted, as much as of the benefit
to the man who gets in; or perhaps we think of it
more.   It suggests to us that one man has been shut
out for the benefit of his neighbour; and that, of
course, suggests envy, malice, and all uncharitable-
ness.   We hold that such competition must generate
ill-will.   I used—when I was intimately connected

with a competitive system at the university—to hear
occasionally of the evil influences of competition, as
tending to promote jealousy between competitors.
I always replied that, so far as my experience went,
the evil was altogether imaginary.   So far from
competition generating ill-will, the keenest competitors were, as a rule, the closest friends.   There
was no stronger bond than the bond of rivalry in
our intellectual contests.   One main reason was,
of course, that we had absolute faith in the fairness
of the competition.   We felt that it would be
unworthy to complain of being beaten by a better
man; and we had no doubt that, in point of fact, the
winners were the better men; or, at any rate, were
honestly believed to be the better men by those
who distributed honours.   The case, though on
a small scale, may suggest one principle.   So far
as the end of such competitions is good, the
normal motives cannot be bad.   The end of a fair
competition is the discovery of the ablest men, with
a view to placing them in the position where their
talents may be turned to most account.   It can only
be achieved so far as each man does his best to train
his own powers, and is prepared to test them fairly
against the powers of others.   To work for that end
is, then, not only permissible, but a duty.   The spirit
in which the end is pursued may be bad, in so far as

a man pursues it by unfair means; in so far as he tries to make sham performance pass off for genuine; or, again, in so far as he sets an undue value upon the reward, as apart from the qualities by which it is gained. But if he works simply with the desire of making the best of himself, and if the reward is simply such a position as may enable him to be most useful to society, the competition which results will be bracing and invigorating, and will appeal to no such motives as can be called, in the bad sense, selfish. He is discharging a function which is useful, it is true, to himself; but which is also intrinsically useful to the whole society. The same principle applies, again, to intellectual activity in general. All genuine thought is essentially useful to mankind. In the struggle to discover truth, even our antagonists are, necessarily, our co-operators. A philosopher, as a man of science, owes, at least, as much to those who differ from him, as to those who agree with him. The conflict of many minds, from many sides, is the essential condition of intellectual progress. Now, if a man plays his part manfully and honourably in such a struggle, he deserves our gratitude, even if he takes the wrong side. If he looks forward to the recognition by the best judges as one motive for his activity, I think that he is asking for a worthy reward. He deserves blame, only

so far as his motives have a mixture of unworthy
personal sentiment.   Obviously, if he aims at cheap
fame, at making a temporary sensation instead of a
permanent impression, at flattering prejudices instead
of spreading truth; or, if he shows greediness of
notoriety, by trying to get unjust credit, as we sometimes see scientific people squabbling over claims to
the first promulgation of some trifling discovery, he
is showing paltriness of spirit.   The men whom we
revere are those who, like Faraday or Darwin, devoted
themselves exclusively to the advancement of knowledge, and would have scorned a reputation won by
anything but genuine work.   The fact that there is
a competition in such matters implies, no doubt, a
temptation,—the temptation to set a higher value
upon praise than upon praiseworthiness; but I think
it not only possible that the competitors in such
rivalries may keep to the honourable path, but
probable that, as a matter of fact, they frequently,—I
hope that I may say generally,—do so.   If the fame
at which a man aims be not that which "in broad
rumour lies," but that which "lives and spreads
aloft in those pure eyes and perfect witness of all-
judging Jove," then I think that the desire for it is
scarcely to be called a last infirmity—rather, it is an
inseparable quality of noble minds.   We wish to
honour men who have been good soldiers in that

warfare, and we can hardly wish them to be indifferent to our homage.

We may add, then, that a competition need not be
demoralising when the competitors have lofty aims
and use only honourable means.   When, passing
from purely intellectual aims, we consider the case,
say, of the race for wealth, we may safely make an
analogous remark.   If a man's aim in becoming rich
is of the vulgar kind; if he wishes to make an
ostentatious display of wealth, and to spend his
money upon demoralising amusement; or if, again,
he tries to succeed by quackery instead of by the
production of honest work, he is, of course, so far
mischievous and immoral.   But a man whose aims
are public-spirited, nay, even if they be such as
simply tend to improve the general comfort; who
develops, for example, the resources of the country,
and introduces new industries or more effective modes
of manufacture, is, undoubtedly, in fact conferring a
benefit upon his fellows, and may, so far, be doing
his duty in the most effectual way open to him.   If
he succeeds by being really a more efficient man of
business than his neighbours, he is only doing what,
in the interests of all, it is desirable that he should
do.   He is discharging an essential social function;
and what is to be desired is, that he should feel the
responsibility involved, that he should regard his

work as on one side the discharge of a social function, and not simply as a means of personal aggrandisement. It is not the fact that he is competing that is against him; but the fact, when it is a fact, that there is something discreditable about the means which he adopts, or the reward that he contemplates.

This, indeed, suggests another and a highly important question—the question, namely, whether, in our present social state, his reward may not be excessive, and won at too great a cost to his rivals. And, without going into other questions involved, I will try to say a little, in conclusion, upon this, which is certainly a pressing problem. Competition, I have suggested, is not immoral if it is a competition in doing honest work by honourable means, and if it is also a fair competition. But it must, of course, be added, that fairness includes more than the simple equality of chances. It supposes, also, that there should be some proportion between the rewards and the merits. If it is simply a question between two men, which shall be captain of a ship, and which shall be mate, then the best plan is to decide by their merits as sailors; and, if their merits be fairly tried, the loser need bear no grudge against the winner. But when we have such cases as sometimes occur, when, for example, the ship is cast away, and it becomes a question whether I shall eat you or you shall

eat me, or, let us say, which of us is to have the last
biscuit, we get one of those terrible cases of temptation in which the strongest social bonds sometimes
give way under the strain. The competition, then,
becomes, in the highest degree, demoralising, and the
struggle for existence resolves itself into a mere un-
scrupulous scramble for life, at any sacrifice of others.
That, it is sometimes said, is a parallel to our social
state at present. If I gave an excessive prize to the
first boy in a school and flogged the second, I should
not be doing justice. If one man is rewarded for a
moderate amount of forethought by becoming a
millionaire, and his unsuccessful rivals punished by
starvation or the workhouse, the lottery of life is not
arranged on principles of justice. A man must be a
very determined optimist if he denied the painful
truth to be found in such statements. He must be
blind to many evils if he does not perceive the danger
of dulling his sympathies by indifference to the fate
of the unsuccessful. The rich man in Clough's poem
observes that, whether there be a God matters very
little—

> For I and mine, thank somebody,
> Manage to get our victual.

But, even if we are not very rich, we must often, I
think, doubt whether we are not wrapping ourselves
in a spirit of selfish complacency when we are

returning to a comfortable home and passing out-
casts of the street.   We must sometimes reflect that
our comfort is not simply a reward for virtue or
intelligence, even if it be not sometimes the prize of
actual dishonesty.   To shut our eyes to the mass of
wretchedness around us is to harden our hearts,
although to open our hands is too often to do more
harm than good.   It is no wonder that we should be
tempted to declaim against competition, when the
competition means that so many unfortunates are to
be crowded off their narrow standing-ground into the
gulf of pauperism.

   This may suggest the moral which I have been
endeavouring to bring out.   Looking at society at
large, we may surely say that it will be better in
proportion as every man is strenuously endeavouring
to play his part, and in which the parts are distributed to those best fitted to play them.   We must
admit, too, that for any period to which we can look
forward, the great mass of mankind will find enough
to occupy their energies in labouring primarily for
their own support, and so bearing the burden of
their own needs and the needs of their families.   We
may infer, too, that a society will be the better so
far as it gives the most open careers to all talents,
wherever displayed, and as it shows respect for the
homely virtues of industry, integrity, and fore-

thought, which are essential to the whole body as to its constituent members. And we may further say that the corresponding motives in the individual cannot be immoral. A desire of independence, the self-respect which makes a man shrink from accepting as a gift what he can win as a fair reward, the love of fairplay, which makes him use only honest means in the struggle, are qualities which can never lose their value, and which are not the less valuable because in the first instance they are most profitable to their possessors. Nothing which tends to weaken such motives can be good; but while they preserve their intensity, they necessarily imply the existence of competition in some form or other.

It is equally clear that competition by itself is not a sufficient panacea. Whenever we take an abstract quality, personify it by the help of capital letters, and lay it down as the one principle of a complex system, we generally blunder. Competition is as far as possible from being the solitary condition of a healthy society. It must be not only a competition for worthy ends by honourable means, but should be a competition so regulated that the reward may bear some proportion to the merit. Monopoly is an evil in so far as it means an exclusive possession of some advantages or privileges, especially when they are given by the accidents of birth or position. It is

something if they are given to the best and the
ablest; but the evil still remains if even the best and
ablest are rewarded by a position which cramps the
energies and lowers the necessity of others. Competition is only desirable in so far as it is a process
by which the useful qualities are encouraged by an
adequate, and not more than an adequate, stimulus ;
and in which, therefore, there is not involved the
degradation and the misery on the one side, the
excessive reward on the other, of the unsuccessful
and the successful in the struggle.   Competition,
therefore, we might say, could be unequivocally
beneficial only in an ideal society ; in a state in which
we might unreservedly devote ourselves to making
the best of our abilities and accepting the consequent
results, without the painful sense in the background
that others were being sacrificed and debased; crushed
because they had less luck in the struggle, and
were, perhaps, only less deserving in some degree
than ourselves.   So long as we are still far enough
from having realised any such state ; so long as we
feel, and cannot but feel, that the distribution of
rewards is so much at the mercy of chance, and so
often goes to qualities which, in an ideal state, would
deserve rather reprobation than applause, we can
only aim at better things.   We can do what in us
lies to level some inequalities, to work, so far as

our opportunities enable us, in the causes which are mostly beneficial for the race, to spread enlightenment and good feeling, and to help the unfortunate. But it is also incumbent upon us to remember carefully, what is so often overlooked in the denunciations of competition, that the end for which we must hope, and the approach to which we must further, is one in which the equivocal virtue of charity shall be suppressed; that is, in which no man shall be dependent upon his neighbour in such a sense as to be able to neglect his own duties; in which there may be normally a reciprocity of good services, and the reciprocity not be (as has been said) all on one side. There is a very explicable tendency at present to ask for such one-sided reciprocity. It is natural enough, for reasons too obvious to be mentioned, that reformers should dwell exclusively upon the right of every one to support, and neglect to point out the correlative duty of every one to do his best to support himself. The popular arguments about "old-age pensions" may illustrate the general state of mind. It is disgraceful, people say, that so large a proportion of the aged poor should come to depend upon the rates. Undoubtedly it is disgraceful. Then upon whom does the disgrace fall? It sounds harsh to say that it falls upon the sufferers. We shrink from saying to a pauper, " It serves you right ".

That sounds brutal, and is only in part true.
Still, we should not shrink from stating whatever is
true, painful though it may be. It sounds better to lay
all the blame upon the oppressor than to lay it upon
the oppressed; and yet, as a rule, the cowardice or
folly of the oppressed has generally been one cause of
their misfortunes, and cannot be overlooked in a true
estimate of the case. That drunkenness, improvidence, love of gambling, and so forth, do in fact lead
to pauperism is undeniable; and that they are bad,
and so far disgraceful, is a necessary consequence.
In such cases, then, pauperism is a proof of bad
qualities; and the fact, like all other facts, must be
recognised. The stress of argument, therefore, is laid
upon the hardships suffered by the honest and industrious poor. The logical consequence should be, that
the deserving poor should become pensioners, and
the undeserving paupers. This at once opens the
amazingly difficult question of moral merit, and the
power of poor-law officials to solve problems which
would certainly puzzle the keenest psychologists.
Suppose, for example, that a man, without being
definitely vicious, has counted upon the promised
pension, and therefore neglected any attempts to save.
If you give him a pension, you virtually tell everybody that saving is a folly; if you don't, you inflict
upon him the stigma which is deserved by the

drunkard and the thief. So difficult is it to arrange
for this proposed valuation of a man's moral qualities
that it has been proposed to get rid of all stigma by
making it the right and duty of every one to take a
pension. That might conceivably alter the praise,
but it would surely not alter the praiseworthiness.
It must be wrong in me to take money from my
neighbours when I don't want it; and, if wrong, it
surely ought to be disgraceful. And this seems to
indicate the real point. We may aim at altering
the facts, at making them more conducive to good
qualities; but we cannot alter or attempt to decide
by laws the degree of praise or blame to be attached
to individuals. It would be very desirable to
bring about a state of things in which no honest
and provident man need ever fall into want; and, in
that state, pauperism would be rightly discreditable as an indication of bad qualities. But to
say that nobody shall be ashamed of taking support
would be to ruin the essential economic virtues, and
to pauperise the nation; and to try to lay down precise rules as to the distribution of honour and discredit, seems, to me, to be a problem beyond the
power of a legislature. I express no opinion upon
the question itself, because I am quite incompetent
to do so. I only refer to it as illustrating the difficulties which beset us when we try to remove the

evils of the present system, and yet to preserve the
stimulus to industry, which is implied in competition. The shortest plan is to shut one's eyes to
the difficulty, and roundly deny its existence. I hope
that our legislators may hit upon some more
promising methods. The ordinary mode of cutting
the knot too often suggests that the actually contemplated ideal is the land in which the chickens run
about ready roasted, and the curse of labour is finally
removed from mankind. The true ideal, surely, is
the state in which labour shall be generally a
blessing; in which we shall recognise the fact—disagreeable or otherwise—that the race can only be
elevated by the universal diffusion of public spirit, and
a general conviction that it is every man's first duty
to cultivate his own capacities, to turn them to
the best possible account, and to work strenuously
and heartily in whatever position he has been placed.
It is because I cannot help thinking that when we
attack competition in general terms, we are, too often,
blinding ourselves to those homely and often-repeated,
and, as I believe, indisputable truths, that I have
ventured to speak to-day, namely, on the side of competition—so far, at least, on the side of competition
as to suggest that our true ideal should be, not a state,
if such a state be conceivable, in which there is no
competition, but a state in which competition should

be so regulated that it should be really equivalent to a process of bringing about the best possible distribution of the whole social forces; and should be held to be, because it would really be, not a struggle of each man to seize upon a larger share of insufficient means, but the honest effort of each man to do the very utmost he can to make himself a thoroughly efficient member of society.

SOCIAL EQUALITY.

THE problem of which I propose to speak is the old
dispute between Dives and Lazarus. Lazarus, presumably, was a better man than Dives. How could
Dives justify himself for living in purple and fine
linen, while Lazarus was lying at the gates, with the
dogs licking his sores? The problem is one of all
ages, and takes many forms. When the old Puritan
saw a man going to the gallows, "There," he said,
"but for the grace of God, goes John Bradford".
When the rich man, entering his club, sees some
wretched tatterdemalion, slouching on the pavement,
there, he may say, goes Sir Gorgius Midas, but for—
what? I am here and he there, he may say, because
I was the son of a successful stock-jobber, and he
the son of some deserted mother at the workhouse.
That is the cause, but is it a reason? Suppose, as
is likely enough, that Lazarus is as good a man as
Midas, ought they not to change places, or to share
their property equally? A question, certainly, to be
asked, and, if possible, to be answered.

It is often answered, and is most simply answered,

by saying that all men ought to be equal. Dives should be cut up and distributed in equal shares between Lazarus and his brethren. The dogma which embodies this claim is one which is easily refuted in some of the senses which it may bear, though in spite of such refutations it has become an essential part of the most genuine creed of mankind. The man of science says, with perfect truth, that so far from men being born equal, some are born with the capacity of becoming Shakespeares and Newtons, and others with scarcely the power of rising above Sally the chimpanzee. The answer would be conclusive, if anybody demanded that we should all be just six feet high, with brains weighing sixty ounces, neither more nor less. It is also true, and, I conceive, more relevant, that, as the man of science will again say, all improvement has come through little groups of men superior to their neighbours, through races or through classes, which, by elevating themselves on the shoulders of others, have gained leisure and means for superior cultivation. But equality may be demanded as facilitating this process, by removing the artificial advantages of wealth. It may be taken as a demand for a fair start, not as a demand that the prizes shall be distributed irrespectively of individual worth. And, whether the demand is rightly or wrongly expressed, we must, I

think, admit that the real force with which we have
to reckon is the demand for justice and for equality
as somehow implied by justice. It is easy to
browbeat a poor man who wants bread and cheese
for himself and his family, by calling his demands
materialistic, and advising him to turn his mind to
the future state, where he will have the best of Dives.
It is equally easy to ascribe the demands to mere
envy and selfishness, or to those evil-minded
agitators who, for their own wicked purposes, induce men to prefer a guinea to a pound of wages.
But, after all, there is something in the demand for
fair play and for the means of leading decent lives,
which requires a better answer. It is easy, again, to
say that all Socialists are Utopian. Make every man
equal to-day, and the old inequalities will reappear
to-morrow. Pitch such a one over London Bridge,
it was said, with nothing on but his breeches, and he
will turn up at Woolwich with his pockets full of gold.
It is as idle to try for a dead level, when you work
with such heterogeneous materials, as to persuade a
homogeneous fluid to stand at anything but a dead
level. But surely it may be urged that this is as
much a reason for declining to believe that equal
conditions of life will produce mere monotony, as for
insisting that equality in any state is impossible. The
present system includes a plan for keeping the scum at

the surface. One of the few lessons which I have
learnt from life, and not found already in copy-books,
is the enormous difficulty which a man of the respectable classes finds in completely ruining himself, even
by vice, extravagance, and folly; whereas, there are
plenty of honest people who, in spite of economy and
prudence, can scarcely keep outside of the workhouse.
Admitting the appeal to justice, it is, again, often
urged that justice is opposed to the demand for
equality. Property is sacred, it is said, because a
man has (or ought to have) a right to what he has
made either by labour or by a course of fair dealings
with other men. I am not about to discuss the
ultimate ground on which the claim to private property is justified, and, as I think, satisfactorily established. A man has a right, we say, to all that he has
fairly earned. Has he, then, a right to inherit what
his father has earned? A man has had the advantage of all that a rich father can do for him in education, and so forth. Why should he also have the
father's fortune, without earning it? Are the merits
of making money so great that they are transmissible
to posterity? Should a man who has been so good
as to become rich, be blessed even to the third and
fourth generation? Why, as a matter of pure justice,
should not all fortunes be applied to public uses, on
the death of the man who made them? Such a law,

however impolitic, would not be incompatible with
the moral principle to which an appeal is made.
There are, of course, innumerable other ways in
which laws may favour an equality of property, without breaking any of the fundamental principles.
What, for example, is the just method of distributing
taxation? A rich man can not only pay more money
than a poor man, in proportion to his income, but he
can, with equal ease, pay a greater proportion. To
double the income of a labourer may be to raise him
from starvation to comfort. To double the income of
a millionaire may simply be to encumber him with
wealth by which he is unable to increase his own
pleasure. There is a limit beyond which it is exceedingly difficult to find ways of spending money on one's
own enjoyment—though I have never been able to
fix it precisely. On this ground, such plans as a
graduated income-tax are, it would seem, compatible
with the plea of justice; and, within certain limits,
we do, in fact, approve of various taxes, on the ground,
real or supposed, that they tend to shift burdens from
the poor to the rich, and, so far, to equalise wealth.
In fact, this appeal to justice is a tacit concession of
the principle. If we justify property on the ground
that it is fair that a man should keep what he has
earned by his own labour, it seems to follow that it is
unjust that he should have anything not earned by

his labour. In other words, the answer admits the ordinary first principle from which Socialism starts, and which, in some Socialist theories, it definitely tries to embody.

All that I have tried to do, so far, is to show that the bare doctrine of equality, which is in some way connected with the demand for justice, is not, of necessity, either unjust or impracticable. It may be used to cover claims which are unjust, to sanction bare confiscation, to take away motives for industry, and, briefly, may be a demand of the drones to have an equal share of the honey. From the bare abstract principle of equality between men, we can, in my own opinion, deduce nothing; and, I do not think that the principle can itself be established. That is why it is made a first principle, or, in other words, one which is not to be discussed. The French revolutionists treated it in this way as *à priori* and self-evident. No school was in more deadly opposition to such *à priori* truths than the school of Bentham and the utilitarians. Yet, Bentham's famous doctrine, that in calculating happiness each man is to count for one, and nobody for more than one, seems to be simply the old principle in a new disguise. James Mill applied the doctrine to politics. J. S. Mill again applied it, with still more thoroughness, especially in his doctrine of representation and of the equality of the sexes. Accordingly, various moralists have urged that this was an inconsistency in utilitarian doctrine, implying that they, too, could make *à priori* first principles when they wanted them. It has become a sort of orthodox dogma with radicals, who do not always trouble themselves about a philosophical basis, and is applied with undoubting confidence to many practical political problems. " One man, one vote " is not simply the formulation of a demand, but seems to intimate a logical ground for the demand. If, in politics, one man is rightfully entitled to one vote, is it not also true that, in economics, one man should have a right to one income, or, that money, like political power, should be distributed into precisely equal shares ? Yet, why are we to take for granted the equality of men in the sense required for such deductions ? Since men are not equally qualified for political power, it would seem better *primâ facie* that each man should have the share of power and wealth which corresponds to his powers of using, or, perhaps, to his powers of enjoying. Why should we not say, " To each man according to his deserts " ? One practical reason, of course, is the extreme difficulty of saying what are the deserts, and how they are to be ascertained. Undoubtedly, equality is the shortest and simplest way ; but, if we take it merely as the most convenient assumption, it loses its attractive appearance of abstract justice or *à priori* self-certainty. Do a common labourer and Mr. Gladstone deserve the same share of voting power?   If not, how many votes should Mr. Gladstone possess to give him his just influence ?   To ask such questions is to show that answering is impossible, though political theorists have, now and then, tried to put together some ostensible pretext for an answer.

What, let us ask, is the true relation between justice and equality?   A judge, to take the typical case, is perfectly just when he ascertains the facts by logical inferences from the evidence, and then applies the law in the spirit of a scientific reasoner. Given the facts, what is the rule under which they come ?   To answer that question, generally speaking, is his whole duty.   In other words, he has to exclude all irrelevant considerations, such as his own private interests or affections.   The parties are to be to him merely A and B, and he has to work out the result as an arithmetician works out a sum.   Among the irrelevant considerations are frequently some moral aspects of the case.   A judge, for example, decides a will to be valid or invalid without asking whether the testator acted justly or unjustly in a moral sense, but simply whether his action was legal or illegal.   He cannot go behind the law, even from motives of benevolence or general maxims of justice, without being an unjust judge. Cases may arise, indeed, as I must say in passing, in which this is hardly true. A law may be so flagrantly unjust that a virtuous judge would refuse to administer it. One striking case was that of the fugitive slave law in the United States, where a man had to choose between acting legally and outraging humanity. So we consider a parent unjust who does not leave his fortune equally among his children. Unless there should be some special reason to the contrary, we shall hold him to be unfair for making distinctions out of mere preference of one child to another. Yet in the case of primogeniture our opinion would have to be modified. Supposing, for example, a state of society in which primogeniture was generally recognised as desirable for public interests, we could hardly call a man unjust for leaving his estates to his eldest son. If, in such a state, a man breaks the general rule, our judgment of his conduct would be determined perhaps by considering whether he was before or behind his age, whether he was acting from a keener perception of the evils of inequality or actuated by spite or regardless of the public interests which he believed to be concerned. A parent treats his children equally in his will in regard to money; but he does not, unless he is a fool, give the same training or the same opening to all his children, whether they are stupid or clever, industrious or idle. But what I wish to insist upon is, that justice implies essentially indifference to irrelevant considerations, and therefore, in many cases, equality in the treatment of the persons concerned. A judge has to decide without reference to bribes, and not be biassed by the position of an accused person. In that sense he treats the men equally, but of course he does not give equal treatment to the criminal and innocent, to the rightful and wrongful claimant.

The equality implied in justice is therefore to be understood as an exclusion of the irrelevant, and thus supposes an understanding as to what is irrelevant. It is not a mere abstract assertion of equality; but the assertion that, in a given concrete case, a certain rule is to be applied without considering anything outside of the rule. An ideally perfect rule would contain within itself a sufficient indication of what is to be relevant. All men of full age, sound mind, and so forth, are to be treated in such and such a way. Then all cases falling within the rule are to be decided on the same principles, and in that sense equally. But the problem remains, what considerations should be taken into account by the rule itself? Let us put the canon of equality in a different

shape, namely, that there should always be a sufficient reason for any difference in the treatment of
our fellows. This rule does not imply that I should
act in all cases as though all men were equal in
character or mind, but that my action should in all
cases be justified by some appropriate consideration.
It does not prove that every man should have a vote,
but that if one man has a vote and another has not,
there should be some adequate reason for the
difference. It does not prove that every man should
work eight hours a day and have a shilling an hour;
but that differences of hours or of pay and, equally,
uniformity of hours and pay, should have some sufficient justification. This is a deeper principle, which
in some cases justifies and in others does not justify
the rule of equality. The rule of equality follows
from it under certain conditions, and has gained
credit because, in point of fact, those conditions have
often been satisfied.

The revolutionary demand for equality was, his-
torically speaking, a protest against arbitrary inequality. It was a protest against the existence of
privileges accompanied by no duties. When the
rich man could only answer the question, "What
have you done to justify your position?" by the
famous phrase of Beaumarchais, "I took the trouble
to be born," he was obviously in a false position.

The demand for a society founded upon reason, in
this sense that a sufficient reason should be given for
all differences, was, it seems to me, perfectly right ;
and, moreover, was enough to condemn the then
established system. But when this demand has been
so constructed as to twist a logical rule, applicable
to all scientific reasoning, into a dogmatic assertion
that certain concrete beings were in fact equal, and
to infer that they should have equal rights, it ceased
to be logical at all, and has been a fruitful parent of
many fallacies. Reasonable beings require a sufficient reason for all differences of conduct, for the
difference between their treatment of a man and a
monkey or a white man and a black, as well as for
differences between treatment of rich and poor or
wise men and fools ; and there must, as the same
principle implies, be also a sufficient reason for
treating all members of a given class equally. We
have to consider whether, for any given purpose, the
differences between human beings and animals,
Englishmen and negroes, men and women, are or
are not of importance for our purpose. When the
differences are irrelevant we neglect them or admit
the claim to equality of treatment. But the question as to relevance is not to be taken for granted
either way. It would be a very convenient but a
very unjustifiable assumption in many cases, as it

might save an astronomer trouble if he assumed that every star was equal to every other star.

The application of this is, I think, obvious. The *à priori* assumption of the equality of men is, in some sense, easily refuted. But the refutation does not entitle us to assume that arbitrary inequality, inequality for which no adequate ground can be assigned, is therefore justifiable. It merely shows that the problem is more complex than has been assumed at first sight. "All men ought to be equal." If you mean equal in natural capacity or character, it is enough to say that what is impossible cannot be. If you propose that the industrious and idle, the good and bad, the wise and foolish, should share equally in social advantages, the reply is equally obvious, that such a scheme, if possible, would be injurious to the qualities on which human welfare depends. If you say that men should be rewarded solely according to their intrinsic merits, we must ask, do you mean to abstract from the adventitious advantages of education, social surroundings, and so forth, or to take men as they actually are, whatever the circumstances to which their development is owing? To ask what a man would have been had he been in a different position from his youth, is to ask for an impossible solution, and one, moreover, of no practical bearing. I shall

not employ a drunkard if I am in want of a butler,
whether he has become a drunkard under over-
powering temptation or become a drunkard from
inherited dipsomania.   But if, on the other hand, I
take the man for what he is, without asking how he
has come to be what he is, I leave the source at least
of all the vast inequalities of which we complain.
The difficulty, which I will not try to develop further,
underlies, as I think, the really vital difference of
method by which different schools attempt to answer
the appeal for social justice.

The school of so-called individualists finds, in fact,
that equality in their sense is incompatible with the
varied differences due to the complete growth of the
social structure.   They look upon men simply as so
many independent units of varying qualities, no
doubt, but still capable of being considered for
political and social purposes as equal.   They ask
virtually what justice would demand if we had before
us a crowd of independent applicants for the good
things of the world, and the simplest answer is to
distribute the good things equally.   If it is replied
that the idle and the industrious should not be upon
the same footing, they are ready to agree, perhaps,
that men should be rewarded according to their
services to society, however difficult it may be to
arrange the proportions.   But it soon appears that

the various classes into which society is actually
divided imply differences not due to the individual
and his intrinsic merits, but to the varying surroundings in which he is placed. To do justice, then, it
becomes necessary to get rid of these differences.
The extreme case is that of the family. Every one
probably owes more to his mother and to his early
domestic environment than to any other of the
circumstances which have influenced his development. If you and I started as perfectly equal babies,
and you have become a saint and I a sinner,
the divergence probably began when our mothers
watched our cradles, and was made inevitable before
we had left their knees. Consequently, the more
thorough-going designers of Utopia have proposed to
abolish this awkward difference.   Men must be
different at their birth ; but we might conceivably
arrange public nurseries which should place them all
under approximately equal conditions.   Then any
differences would result from a man's intrinsic qualities, and he might be said to be rewarded simply
according to his own merits.

The plan may be tempting, but has its disadvan-
tages.   There are injustices, if we call all inequality
injustice, which we can only attribute to nature or to
the unknown power which makes men and monkeys,
Shakespeares and Stephens.   And one result is that

the character and conduct of human beings depend
to a great extent upon circumstances, which are acci-
dental in the sense that they are circumstances other
than the original endowment of the individual.   In
this sense, maternal love, for example, is unjust.
The mother loves her child because it is her own,
not because it is better (though of course it is better)
than other children.   So, as Adam Smith, I think,
observed, we are more moved by our neighbour's
suffering from a corn on his great toe than by the
starvation of millions in China.   In other words, the
affections, which are the great moving forces of
society, are unjust in so far as they cause us to be
infinitely more interested in our own little circle
than in the remoter members of humanity known to
us only by report.   Without discussing the "justice"
of this arrangement, we shall have, I think, to admit
that it is inevitable.   For I, at least, hold that the
vague and vast organism of humanity depends for its
cohesion upon the affinities and attractions, and not
vice versâ.   My interests are strongest where my
power of action is greatest.   The love of mothers for
children is a force of essential value, and therefore
to be cultivated rather than repressed, for no force
known to us could replace it.   And what is pre-
eminently true in this case is, of course, true to a
degree in others.   Burke stated this with admirable

force in his attack upon the revolutionists who
expounded the opposite principle of abstract equality.
" To be attached to the subdivision, to love the little
platoon we belong to in society, is the first principle," he says, "the germ, as it were, of public
affections. It is the first link in the series by which
we proceed towards a love to our country and mankind." The assertion that they desired to invert this
order, to destroy every social link in so far as it
tended to produce inequalities, was the pith of his
great indictment against the French "metaphysical"
revolutionists. They had perverted the general
logical precept of the sufficient reason for all inequalities by converting it into an assuming of the
equality of concrete units. They fell into the fallacy
of which I have spoken; and many radicals, utilitarians, and others have followed them. They
assumed that all the varieties of human character, or
all those due to the influence of the social environment, through whose structure and inherited instincts
every full-grown man has been moulded, might be
safely disregarded for the purpose of political and
social construction. They have spoken, in brief, as if
men were the equal and homogeneous atoms of
physical inquiry and social problems capable of solution by a simple rearrangement of the atoms in different orders, instead of remembering that they are

dealing with a complex organism, in which not only
the whole order but every constituent atom is also a
complex structure of indefinitely varying qualities.
In the recognition of this truth lies, as I believe, the
true secret of any satisfactory method of treatment.

Does this fact justify inequality in general? Or
does not the principle of equality still remain as
essentially implied in the Utopia which we all desire
to construct? We have to take it for granted that
to each man the first and primary moving instinct is
and must be the love of the little "platoon" of which
he is a member; that the problem is, not to destroy
all these minor attractions, to obliterate the structure
and replace society by a vast multitude of independent atoms, each supposed to aim directly at the
good of the whole, but so to harmonise and develop
or restrain the smaller interests of families, of
groups and associations, that they may spontaneously
co-operate towards the general welfare. It is a long
and difficult task to which we have to apply ourselves; a task not to be effected by the demonstration or application of a single abstract dogma, but to
be worked out gradually by the co-operation of many
classes and of many generations. If it is fairly
solved in the course of a thousand years or so, I for
one shall be very fairly satisfied. But distant as the
realisation may be, we may or rather ought to con-

sider seriously the end to which we should be working. The conception implies a distinction of primary importance towards any clear treatment of the problem. We have, that is, two different, though not altogether distinct, provinces of what I may, perhaps, call organic and functional morality. We may take the existing order for granted, and ask what is then our duty; or we may ask how far the structure itself requires modification, and, if so, what kind of modification. A man who assumes the existence of the present structure may act justly or unjustly within the limits so prescribed. He must generally be guided in a number of cases by some principle of equality. The judge should endeavour to give the same law to rich and poor; the parent should not make arbitrary distinctions between his children; the statesman should try to distribute his burdens without favouring one particular class, and so forth. A man who, in such a sense, acts justly may be described as up to the level of his age and its accepted established moral ideas, and is, therefore, entitled at least to the negative praise of not being corrupt or dishonest. He fulfils accurately the functions imposed upon him, and is not governed by what Bentham called the sinister interests which would prevent them from being effectually discharged for the welfare of the community. But the

problem which we have to consider is the deeper and
more difficult one of organic justice; and our question is what justice means in this case, or what are
the irrelevant considerations to be excluded from our
motives of conduct.

Between these two classes of justice there are
distinctions which it is necessary to state briefly.
Justice, as we generally use the word, implies that
the unjust man deserves to be hanged, or, at least, is
responsible for his actions. What "responsibility"
precisely implies is, of course, a debatable question.
I only need assume that, in any case, it implies that
somebody is guilty of wrong-doing, for which he
should receive an appropriate penalty. But in
organic questions it is not the individual, but the
race which is responsible; and we require a reform,
not a penalty. An impatient temper leads us to
generalise too hastily from the case of the individual
to that of the country. We bestow the blame for all
the wrongs of an oppressed nation, for example, upon
the nation which oppresses. But in simple point of
fact, the oppressed nation generally deserves (if the
word can be fairly used) to share the blame. The
trodden worm would not have been trodden upon if
it had been a bit of a viper. Whatever the duty of
turning the second cheek, it is clearly not a national
duty. If we admire a Tell or Robert Bruce for

resisting oppressors, we implicitly condemn those who submitted to oppressors. If a nation is divided or wanting in courage, public spirit, and independence, it will be trampled down ; and though we may most rightfully blame the tramplers, it is idle to exonerate the trampled. It is easy, in the same way, to make the rich solely responsible for all the misery of the poor. The man who has got the booty is naturally regarded as the robber. But, speaking scientifically, that is, with the desire to state the plain facts, we must admit that if the poor are those who have gone to the wall in the struggle for wealth ; then, whatever unjust weapons have been used in that struggle, the improvidence and vice and idleness have certainly been among the main causes of defeat. Here, as before, the question is not, who is to be punished ? We can only settle that when dealing with individual cases. It is the question, what is the cause of certain evils ? and here we must resist the temptation of supposing that the class which in some sense appears to profit by them, or, at least, to be exempt from them, has, therefore, any more to do with bringing them about than the class which suffers from them.

The reflection may put us in mind of what seems to be a general law. The ultimate cause of the adoption of institutions and rules of conduct is often the fact of their utility to the race ; but it is only at a later period that their utility becomes the conscious or avowed reason for maintaining them. The political fabric has been clearly built up, in great part, by purely selfish ambition. Nations have been formed by energetic rulers, who had no eye for anything beyond the gratification of their own ambition, although they were clear-headed enough to see that their own ambition could best secure its objects by taking the side of the stronger social forces, and by giving substantial benefit to others. The same holds good pre-eminently of industrial relations. We all know how Adam Smith, sharing the philosophical optimism of his time, showed how the pursuit of his own welfare by each man tended, by a kind of pre-ordained harmony, to contribute to the welfare of all. Since his time we have ceased to be so optimistic, and have recognised the fact that the building up of modern industrial systems has involved much injury to large classes. And yet we may, I think, in great measure adopt his view. The fact that each man was rogue enough to think first of himself and of his own wife and family is not a proof or a presumption that he did not flourish because, in point of fact, he was contributing (quite unintentionally perhaps) to the comforts of mankind in general. What we have to reflect is that, while the bare existence of certain

institutions gives a strong presumption of their
utility, there is also a probability that when the
utility becomes a conscious aim or a consciously
adopted criterion of their advantage, they will require
a corresponding modification intended to secure the
advantages at a minimum cost of evil.

Premising these remarks as to the meaning of
organic justice, we can now come to the question
of equality.   Justice in its ordinary sense may be
regarded from one point of view as the first condition
of the efficiency of the social organ.   In saying that
a judge is just, we imply that he is so far efficiently
discharging his part in society—the due application
of the law—without reference to irrelevant considerations.   He is a machine which rightly parts
the sheep and goats—taking the legal definition of
goats and sheep—instead of putting some goats into
the sheepfold, and *vice versâ*.   That is, he secures
the accurate application of the purely legal rule.
Organic justice involves an application of the same
principle because it equally depends upon the exclusion of irrelevant considerations.   It implies such a
distribution of functions and of maintenance as may
secure the greatest possible efficiency of society
towards some end in itself good.   Society of course
may be organised with great efficiency for bad or
doubtful ends.   A purely military organisation, how-

ever admirable for its purpose, may imply a sacrifice
of the highest welfare of the nation. Assuming,
however, the goodness of the end, the greatest efficiency is of course desirable. We may, for our
purposes, assume that the efficiency of a nation
regarded as a society for the production of wealth is
a desirable end. There are, of course, many other
purposes which must not be sacrificed to the production of wealth. But power of producing wealth,
meaning roughly whatever contributes to the physical
support and comfort of the nation, is undoubtedly a
necessary condition of all other happiness. If we all
starve we can have neither art nor science nor
morality. What I mean, therefore, is that a nation
is so far better as it is able to raise all necessary
supplies with the least expenditure of labour, leaving
aside the question how far the superfluous forces
should be devoted to raising comparative luxuries or
to some purely religious or moral or intellectual
purposes. The perfect industrial organisation is, I
shall assume, compatible with or rather a condition
of a perfect organisation of other kinds. In the most
general terms we have to consider what are the principles of social organisation, which of course implies
a certain balance between the various organs and a
thorough nutrition of all, while yet we may for a
moment confine our attention to the purely industrial

or economic part of the question. How, if at all, does the principle of equality or of social justice enter the problem?

We may assume, in the the first place, from this point of view, that one most obvious condition is the absence of all purely useless structures, whether of the kind which we call "survivals" or such as may be called parasitic growths. The organ which has ceased to discharge corresponding functions is simply a drag upon the vital forces. When a class, such as the old French aristocracy, ceases to perform duties while retaining privileges, it will be removed,—too probably, as in that case, it will be removed by violent and mischievous methods,—if the society is to grow in vigour. The individuals, as I have said, may or may not deserve punishment, for they are not personally responsible for the general order of things; but they are not unlikely to incur severe penalties, and what we should really hope is that they may be in some way absorbed by judicious medical treatment, instead of extirpated by the knife. At the other end of the scale, we have the parasitic class of the beggars or thieves. They, too, are not personally responsible for the conditions into which they are born. But they are not only to be pitied individually, but to be regarded, in the mass, as involving social disease and danger. More words upon that topic are quite super-

fluous, but I may just recall the truth that the two
evils are directly connected. We hear it often said,
and often denied, that the rich are growing richer
and the poor poorer. So far, however, as it is true,
it is one version of the very obvious fact that where
there are many careless rich people, there will be the
best chance for the beggars. The thoughtless expenditure of the rich without due responsibilities,
provides the steady stream of so-called charity,—the
charity which, as Shakespeare (or somebody else)
observes, is twice cursed, which curses him that gives
and him that receives; which is to the rich man as a
mere drug to still his conscience and offer a spurious
receipt in full for his neglect of social duties, and to
the poor man an encouragement to live without self-
respect, without providence, a mere hanger-on and
dead-weight upon society, and a standing injury and
source of temptation to his honest neighbours.

Briefly, a wholesome social condition implies that
every social organ discharges a useful function; it
renders some service to the community which is
equivalent to the support which it derives; brain and
stomach each get their due share of supply; and
there is a thorough reciprocity between all the different members of the body. But what kind of equality
should be desired in order to secure this desirable
organic balance? We have to do, I may remark,

with the case of a homogeneous race. By this I mean not only that there is no reason to suppose that there is any difference between the innate qualities of rich and poor, but that there is the strongest reason for believing in an equality; that is to say, more definitely, that if you took a thousand poor babies and a thousand rich babies, and subjected them to the same conditions, they would show great individual differences, but no difference traceable to the mere difference of class origin. I therefore may leave aside such problems as might arise in the Southern States of America, or even in British India, where two different races are in presence ; or, again, the case of the sexes, where we cannot assume as self-evident, that the organic differences are irrelevant to political or social ends. So far as we are concerned, we may take it for granted that the differences which emerge are not due to any causes antecedent to and overriding the differences due to different social positions. If we can say justly (as has been said) that a poor man is generally more charitable in proportion to his means, or, again, that he is, as a rule, a greater liar or a greater drunkard than the rich man, the difference is not due to a difference of breed, but to the education (in the widest sense) which each has received. So long as that difference remains, we must take account of it for purposes of obtaining the maximum efficiency. We must not make the poor man a professor of mathematics, or even manager of a railway, because he has talents which, if trained, would have qualified him for the post; but we may and must assume that an equal training would do as much for the poor man as for the rich; and the question is, how far it is desirable or possible to secure such equality.

Now, from the point of view of securing a maximum efficiency, it seems to be a clearly desirable end that the only qualities which should indisputably help to determine a man's position in life, should also be those which determine his fitness for working in it efficiently. In Utopia, it should be the rule that each man shall do what he can do best. If one man is a gamekeeper and another a prime minister, it should be because one has the gifts of a gamekeeper and the other the gifts of a prime minister: whereas, in the actual state, as we all know, the gamekeeper often becomes the prime minister, while the potential prime minister is limited to looking after poachers. But I also urge that we must take into account the actual and not the potential qualities at any given moment. The inequality may be obviated by raising the grade of culture in all classes; but we must not assume that there is an actual equality where, in fact, there is the widest

possible difference. In short, I assert that it is our
duty to try to make men equal; though I deny that
we are clearly justified in assuming an equality. By
making them equal, I do not, of course, mean that
we should try to make them all alike. I recognise,
with Mill and every sensible writer on the subject,
that such a consummation represents rather a danger
than an advantage. I wish to see individuality
strengthened, not crushed, to encourage men to develop the widest possible diversity of tastes, talents,
and pursuits, and to attain unity of opinion, not by a
calm assumption that this or that creed is true, but
by encouraging the sharpest and freest collision of
opinions. The equality of which I speak is that
which would result, if the distinction into organs
were not of such a nature as to make one class more
favourable than another to the full development of
whatever character and talents a man may possess.
In other words, the distribution into classes would
correspond purely and simply to the telling off of
each man to the duties which he is best fitted to discharge. The position into which he is born, the class
surroundings which determine his development, must
not carry with them any disqualification for his
acquiring the necessary aptitude for any other position. It was, I think, Fourier who argued that a man
ought to be paid more highly for being a chimney-

sweep than for being a prime minister, because the
duties of a sweep are the more disagreeable,—a position which some prime ministers may, perhaps, see
reason to doubt. My suggestion is, that in Utopia
every human being would be so placed as to be
capable of preparing himself for any other position,
and should then go to the work for which he is best
fitted. The equality as thus defined would, I submit,
leave no room for a sense of injustice, because the
qualities which determine a man's position would be
the qualities for which he deserves the position, desert in this sense being measurable by fitness. Discontent with class distinctions must arise so long as
a man feels that his position in a class limits and
cramps his capacities below the level of happier
fortunes. Discontent is not altogether a bad thing,
for it is often an *alias* for hope ; remove all discontent
and you remove all guarantee for improvement.
But discontent is of the malignant variety when it is
allied with a sense of injustice ; that is, of restrictions
imposed upon one class for no assignable reason.
The only sufficient reason for classes is the efficient
discharge of social functions. The differences between the positions of men in social strata, supply
some of the most effective motives for the struggle of
life ; and the effort of men to rise into the wealthy or
the powerful class is not likely to cease so long as

men are men; but they take an unworthy form so long
as the ambition is simply to attain privileges uncon-
nected with or disproportioned to the duties involved,
and which therefore generate hatred to the social
structure. If a class could be simply an organ for
the discharge of certain functions, and each man in
the whole body politic able to fit himself for that class,
the injustice, and therefore the malignant variety of
discontent, would disappear. Of course, I am speaking only of justice. I do not attempt to define the
proper ends of society, or regard justice in itself as a
sufficient guarantee for all desirable results. Such
justice may exist even in a savage tribe or a low
social type. There may be a just distribution of food
among a shipwrecked crew, but the attainment of
such justice would not satisfy all their wants. The
abolition of misery, the elevation of a degraded class
to a higher stage is a good thing in itself, unless it
can be shown to involve some counterbalancing evil.
I only argue that the ideal society would have this,
among other attributes, and, therefore, that to secure
such equality is a legitimate object of aspiration.

I am speaking of "Utopia". The time is indefinitely distant when a man will choose to be a sweep
or a prime minister according to his aptitudes, and
be equally able to learn his trade whether he is the
son of a prime minister or a sweep. I only try to

indicate the goal to which our efforts should be directed. But the goal thus defined implies methods different from that of some advocates of equality. They propose at once to assume the non-existence of a disagreeable difficulty, and to take men as equal in a sense in which they are not, in fact, equal. To me the problem appears to be, not the instant introduction of a new system, but a necessarily long and very gradual process of education directed towards the distant goal of making men equal in the desirable sense; and that problem, I add, is in the main a moral problem. It is idle to make institutions without making the qualities by which they must be worked. I do not say—far from it—that we are not to propose what may roughly be called external changes: new regulations and new forms of association, and so forth. On the contrary, I believe, as I have intimated, that this method corresponds to the normal order of development. The new institution protects and stimulates the germs of the moral instincts by which it must be worked. But I also hold that no mere rearrangement does any permanent good unless it calls forth a corresponding moral change, and, moreover, that the moral change, however slow and imperceptible, does incomparably more than any external change.

If we assume our present institutions to be permanent, a slight improvement in moral qualities, a growth of sobriety, of chastity, of prudence and intellectual culture, would make an almost indefinite improvement in the condition of the masses. If, for example, Englishmen ceased to drink, every English home might be made reasonably comfortable. The two kinds of change imply each other; but it is the most characteristic error of the designers of Utopias to suppose a mere change of regulations without sufficiently attending to the moral implication. To attain equality, as I have tried to define the word, would imply vast moral changes, and therefore a long and difficult elaboration. We have not simply to make men happy, as they now count happiness, but to alter their views of happiness. The good old copy-books tell us that happiness is as common in poor men's huts as in rich men's palaces. We are apt to reply that the statement is a mockery and a lie. But it points to the consummation which in some simple social states has been partly realised, and which in some distant future may come to be an expression of facts. It is conceivable surely that rich men may some day find that there are modes of occupation which are more interesting as well as more useful than accumulation of luxuries or the keeping of horses for the turf; that, in place of propitiating fate by supporting the institution of beggary, there is an indefinite field for public-spirited energy in the way not of throwing crumbs to Lazarus, but of promoting national culture of mind, of spirit, and of body; that benevolence does not mean simple self-sacrifice, except to the selfish, but the pursuit of a noble and most interesting career; that men's duty to their children is not to enable them to lead idle lives, but to fit them for playing a manly part in the great game of life; and that their relation to those whom they employ is not that of persons exploiting the energies of inferior animals, but of leaders of industry with a common interest in the prosperity of their occupation. People, no doubt, will hardly pursue business from motives of pure benevolence to others, and I do not think it desirable that they should. But the recognition that the pursuit of an honourable business is useful to others may, nevertheless, guide their energies, make the mere scramble for wealth disreputable, and induce them to labour for solid and permanent advantages. Such moral changes are, I conceive, necessary conditions of the equality of which I have spoken; they must be brought about to some extent if the industrial organism is to free itself from the injustice necessarily implied in a mere blind struggle for personal comfort.

Moreover, however distant the final consummation

may be, there are, I think, many indications of an approximation. Nothing is more characteristic of modern society than the enormous development of the power of association for particular purposes. In former days a society had to form an independent organ, a corporation, a college, and so forth, to discharge any particular function, and the resulting organ was so distinct as to absorb the whole life of its members. The work of the fellow was absorbed in the corporate life of his corporation, and he had no distinct personal interests. Now we are all members of societies by the dozen, and society is constantly acquiring the art of forming associations for any purpose, temporary or permanent, which imply no deep structural division, and unite people of all classes and positions. As the profounder lines are obliterated, the tendency to form separate castes, defended by personal privileges, and holding themselves apart from other classes, rapidly diminishes; and the corresponding prejudices are in process of diminution. But I can only hint at this principle.

A correlative moral change in the poor is, of course, equally essential. America is described by Mr. Lowell in the noblest panegyric ever made upon his own country, as " She that lifts up the manhood of the poor ". She has taken some rather queer

methods of securing that object lately; yet, however
imperfect the result, every American traveller will, I
believe, sympathise with what Mr. Bryce has recently
said in his great book. America is still the land of
hope—the land where the poor man's horizon is not
bounded by a vista of inevitable dependence on
charity; where—in spite of some superficially gro-
tesque results—every man can speak to every other
without the oppressive sense of condescension;
where a civil word from a poor man is not always a
covert request for a gratuity and a tacit confession of
dependence. "Alas," says Wordsworth, in one of
his pregnant phrases, "the gratitude of men has
oftener left me mourning" than their cold-hearted-
ness; because, I presume, it is a painful proof of
the rarity of kindness. When one man can only
receive a gift and another can only bestow it as a
payment on account of a long accumulation of the
arrears of class injustice, the relations hardly admit
of genuine gratitude on either side. What grates
most painfully upon me, and, I suppose, upon most
of us, is the "servility" of man; the acceptance of a
beggar's code of morals as natural and proper for
any one in a shabby coat. The more prominent evil
just now, according to conservatives and pessimists,
is the correlative one of the beggar on horseback; of
the man who has found out that he can squeeze

more out of his masters, and uses his power even
without considering whether it is wise to drain your
milch cow too exhaustively.

A hope of better things is encouraged by schemes
for arbitration and conciliation between employers
and employed. But we require a moral change if
arbitration is tu imply something more than a truce
between natural enemies, and conciliation to be
something different from that employed by Hood's
butcher when, after hauling a sheep by main force
into the slaughter-house, he exclaimed, " There, I've
conciliated *him!*" The only principle on which
arbitration can proceed is that the profits should be
divided in such a way as to be a sufficient inducement to all persons concerned to give their money
or their labour, mental or physical, to promote the
prosperity of the business at large. But the reconciliation can only be complete when the capitalist is
capable of employing his riches with enough public
spirit and generosity to disarm mere envy by his
obvious utility, and the poor man justifies his increased wages by his desire to secure permanent
benefits and a better standard of life. In Utopia, the
question will still be, what plan shall be a sufficient
inducement to the men who co-operate as employers
or labourers, but the inducement will appeal to better
motives, and the positions be so far equalised that

each will be most tolerable to the man best fitted for it.

Here a vast series of problems opens about which I can only suggest the briefest hint. The principle I now urge is the old one, namely, that the usual mark of a quack remedy is the neglect of the moral aspect of a question. We want a state of opinion in which the poor are not objects to be slobbered over, but men to help in a manly struggle for moral as well as material elevation. A great deal is said, for example, about the evils of competition. It is remarkable indeed that few proposals for improvement even, so far as I can discover, tend to get rid of competition. Co-operation, as tradesmen will tell us, is not an abolition of competition, but a competition of groups instead of units. "Profit-sharing" is simply a plan by which workmen may take a direct share in the competition carried on by their masters. I do not mention this as any objection to such schemes, for I do not think that competition is an evil. I do not doubt the vast utility of schemes which tend to increase the intelligence and prudence of workmen, and give them an insight into the conditions of successful business. Competition is no doubt bad so far as it means cheating or gambling. But competition is, it seems to me, inevitable so long as we are forced to apply the experimental method in practical life, and I fail to see what other method is available. Competition means that thousands of people all over the world are trying to find out how they can supply more economically and efficiently the wants of other people, and that is a state of things to which I do not altogether object. Equality in my sense implies that every one should be allowed to compete for every place that he can fill. The cry is merely, as it seems to me, an evasion of the fundamental difficulty. That difficulty is not that people compete, but that there are too many competitors; not that a man's seat at the table has to be decided by fair trial of his abilities, but that there is not room enough to seat everybody. Malthus brought to the front the great stumbling-block in the way of Utopian optimism. His theory was stated too absolutely, and his view of the remedy was undoubtedly crude. But he hit the real difficulty; and every sensible observer of social evils admits that the great obstacle to social improvement is that social residuum, the parasitic class, which multiplies so as to keep down the standard of living, and turns to bad purposes the increased power of man over nature. We have abolished pestilence and famine in their grimmest shape; if we have not abolished war, it no longer involves usurpation or slavery or the permanent desolation of the conquered; but one result is just this, that great masses can be regularly kept alive at the lowest stage of existence without being periodically swept away by a "black death" or a horde of brutal invaders. If we choose to turn our advantages to account in this way, no nostrums will put an end to poverty; and the evil can only be met—as I venture to assume—by an elevation of the moral level, involving all that is implied in spreading civilisation downward.

The difficulty shows itself in discussions of the proper sphere of government. Upon that vast and most puzzling topic I will only permit myself one remark. In former times the great aim of reformers was the limitation of the powers of government. They came to regard it as a kind of bogy or extra-natural force, which acted to oppress the poor in order to maintain certain personal privileges. Some, like Godwin of the "Political Justice," held that the millennium implied the abolition of government and the institution of anarchy. The early utilitarians held that government might be reformed by placing power in the hands of the subjects, who would use it only for their own interests, but still retained the prejudices engendered in their long struggle against authority, and held that its functions should still be gradually restricted on pain of developing a worse tyranny than the old. The government has been handed over to the people as they desired, but with the natural result that the new authorities not only use it to support their interests, but retain the conviction of its extra-natural, or perhaps supernatural, efficacy. It is regarded as an omnipotent body which can not only say (as it can) that whatever it pleases shall be legal, but that whatever is made a law in the juridical sense shall at once become a law of nature. Even their individualist opponents, who profess to follow Mr. Herbert Spencer, seem often to regard the power of government, not as one result of evolution, but as something external which can constrain and limit evolution. It corresponds to a kind of outside pressure which interferes arbitrarily with the so-called natural course of development, and should therefore be abolished. To me, on the contrary, it seems that government is simply one of the social organs, with powers strictly limited by its relation to others and by the nature of the sentiment upon which it rests. There are obvious reasons, in the centralisation of vast industrial interests, the "integration," as Mr. Spencer calls it, which is the correlative of differentiation, in the growing solidarity of different classes and countries, in the consequent growth of natural monopolies, which give a solid reason for believing that the functions of the central government may require expansion. To decide by

any *à priori* principle what should be the limits of
this expansion is, to my mind, hopeless. The problem is one to be worked out by experiment,—that
is, by many generations and by repeated blundering.
A fool, said Erasmus Darwin, is a man who never
makes an experiment; an experiment is a new mode
of action which fails in its object ninety-nine times
out of a hundred; therefore, wise men make more
blunders, though they also make more discoveries
than fools. Now, experiments in government and
social organisation are as necessary to improvement
as any other kind of experiment, and probably still
more liable to failure. One thing, however, is again
obvious. The simple remedy of throwing everything
upon government, of allowing it to settle the rate of
wages, the hours of labour, the prices of commodities,
and so forth, requires for success a moral and intellectual change which it is impossible to over-
estimate. I will not repeat the familiar arguments
which, to my mind, justify this statement. It is
enough to say that there is no ground in the bare
proposal for putting all manner of industrial regulations into the hands of government, for supposing
that it would not drag down every one into pauperism
instead of raising everybody to comfort. I often read
essays of which the weakness seems to be that while
they purpose to establish equality, they give no real

reason for holding that it would not be an equality of beggary. If every one is to be supported, idle or not, the natural conclusion is universal pauperism. If people are to be forced to work by government, or their numbers to be somehow restricted by government, you throw a stress upon the powers of government which, I will not say, it is impossible that it should bear, but which, to speak in the most moderate terms, implies a complete reconstruction of the intelligence, morality, and conceptions of happiness of human beings. Your government would have to be omniscient and purely benevolent as well as omnipotent, and I confess that I cannot see in the experience of those countries where the people have the most direct influence upon the government, any promise that this state of things will be realised just yet.

Thus, I return to my conclusion,—to my platitude, if you will. Professor Fawcett used to say that he could lay down no rules for the sphere of government influence, except this rule, that no interference would do good unless it helped people to help themselves. I think that the doctrine was characteristic of his good sense, and I fully subscribe to it. I heartily agree that equality in the sense I have given, is a most desirable ideal; I agree that we should do all that in us lies to promote it; I only say that our

aims should be always in consistence with the principle that such equality is only possible and desirable
in so far as the lowest classes are lifted to a higher
standard, morally as well as physically. Of course,
that implies approval of every variety of new institutions and laws, of co-operation, of profit sharing, of
boards of conciliation, of educational and other bodies
for carrying light into darkness and elevating popular
standards of life: but always with the express condition that no such institution is really useful except
as it tends to foster a genuine spirit of independence,
and to supply the moral improvement without which
no outward change is worth a button.   This is a
truism, you may say. Yet, when I read the proposals
to get rid of poverty by summarily ordering people to
be equal, or to extirpate pauperism by spending a
million upon certain institutions for out-door relief,
I cannot help thinking that it is a truism which requires to be enforced. The old Political Economy,
you say, is obsolete; meaning, perhaps, that you do
not mean to be bothered with its assertions; but the
old Economists had their merits. They were among
the first who realised the vast importance of deeper
social questions; they were the first who tried to
treat them scientifically; they were not (I hope) the
last who dared to speak unpleasant truths, simply
because they believed them and believed in their im-

portance. Perhaps, indeed, they rather enjoyed the practice a little too much, and indulged in it a little too ostentatiously. Yet, I am sure that, on the whole, it was a very useful practice, and one which is now scarcely as common as it should be. People are more anxious to pick holes in their statement of economic laws than to insist upon the essential fact that, after all, there are laws, not " laws " made by Parliament, but laws of nature, which do, and will, determine the production and distribution of wealth, and the recognition of which is as important to human welfare as the recognition of physiological laws to the bodily health. Holding this faith, the old Economists were never tired of asserting what is the fundamental truth of so-called " individualism," that, after all we may say about the social development, the essential condition of all social improvement is not that we should have this or that system of regulations, but that the individual should be manly, self-respecting, doing his duty as well as getting his pay, and deeply convinced that nothing will do any permanent good which does not imply the elevation of the individual in his standards of honesty, independence, and good conduct. We can only say to Lazarus : " You are probably past praying for, and all we can do is to save you from starving, by any means which do not encourage other people to fall

into your weaknesses; but we recognise the right of
your class for any and every possible help that can
be given towards making men of them, and putting
them on their legs by teaching them to stand up-
right".

ETHICS AND THE STRUGGLE FOR EXISTENCE.

In his deeply-interesting Romanes lecture, Professor Huxley has stated the opinion that the ethical progress of society depends upon our combating the "cosmic process" which we call the struggle for existence. Since, as he adds, we inherit the "cosmic nature" which is the outcome of millions of years of severe training, it follows that the "ethical nature" may count upon having to reckon with a tenacious and powerful enemy as long as the world lasts. This is not a cheerful prospect. It is, as he admits, an audacious proposal to pit the microcosm against the macrocosm. We cannot help fearing that the microcosm may get the worst of it. Professor Huxley has not fully expanded his meaning, and says much to which I could cordially subscribe. But I think that the facts upon which he relies admit or require an interpretation which avoids the awkward conclusion.

Pain and suffering, as Professor Huxley tells us, are always with us, and even increase in quantity and intensity as evolution advances. The fact had been recognised in remote ages long before theories of evolution had taken their modern form. Pessimism, from the time of the ancient Hindoo philosophers to the time of their disciple, Schopenhauer, has been in no want of evidence to support its melancholy conclusions. It would be idle to waste rhetoric in the attempt to recapitulate so familiar a position. Though I am not a pessimist, I cannot doubt that there is more plausibility in the doctrine than I could wish. Moreover, it may be granted that any attempt to explain or to justify the existence of evil is undeniably futile. It is not so much that the problem cannot be answered, as that it cannot even be asked in any intelligible sense. To "explain" a fact is to assign its causes—that is, to give the preceding set of facts out of which it arose. However far we might go backwards, we should get no nearer to perceiving any reason for the original fact. If we explain the fall of man by Adam's eating the apple, we are quite unable to say why the apple should have been created. If we could discover a general theory of pain, showing, say, that it implied certain physiological conditions, we shall be no nearer to knowing why those physiological conditions should have been what they are. The existence of pain, in short, is one of the primary data of our problem, not one of the accidents, for which we can hope in any intelligible sense to account. To give any "justification" is equally impossible. The book of Job really suggests an impossible, one may almost say a meaningless, problem. We can give an intelligible meaning to a demand for justice when we can suppose that a man has certain antecedent rights, which another man may respect or neglect. But this has no meaning as between the abstraction "nature" and the concrete facts which are themselves nature. It is unjust to meet equal claims differently. But it is not "unjust" in any intelligible sense that one being should be a monkey and another a man, any more than that part of me should be a hand and another head. The question would only arise if we supposed that the man and the monkey had existed before they were created, and had then possessed claims to equal treatment. The most logical theologians, indeed, admit that as between creature and creator there can be properly no question of justice. The pot and the potter cannot complain of each other. If the writer of Job had been able to show that the virtuous were rewarded and the vicious punished, he would only have transferred the problem to another issue. The judge might be justified, but the creator would be condemned. How can it be just to place a being where he is certain to sin, and then to damn him for sinning? That is the problem to which no answer can be given; and which already implies a confusion of ideas. We apply the conception of justice in a sphere where it is not applicable, and naturally fail to get any intelligible answer.

It is impossible to combine the conceptions of God as the creator and God as the judge; and the logical straits into which the attempt leads are represented by the endless free-will controversy. I will not now enter that field of controversy: and I will only indicate what seems to me to be the position which we must accept in any scientific discussion of our problem. Hume, as I think, laid down the true principle when he said that there could be no *à priori* proof of a matter of fact. An *à priori* truth is a truth which cannot be denied without self-contradiction, but there can never be a logical consideration in supposing the non-existence of any fact whatever. The ordinary appeal to the truths of pure mathematics is, therefore, beside the question. All such truths are statements of the precise equivalence of two propositions. To say that there are four things is also to say that there are two pairs of things: to say that there is a plane triangle is also to say that there is a plane trilateral. One statement involves the other, because the difference is not in the thing described, but in our mode of contemplating it. We, therefore, cannot make one assertion and deny the other without implicit contradiction. From such results, again, is evolved (in the logical sense of evolution) the whole vast system of mathematical truths. The complexity of that system gives the erroneous idea that we can, somehow, attain a knowledge of facts, independently of experience. We fail to observe that even the most complex mathematical formula is simply a statement of an exact equivalence of two assertions; and that, till we know by experience the truth of one statement, we can never infer the truth, in fact, of the other. However elaborate may be the evolutions of mathematical truth, they can never get beyond the germs out of which they are evolved. They are valid precisely because the most complex statement is always the exact equivalent of the simpler, out of which it is constructed. They remain to the end truths of number or truths of geometry. They cannot, by themselves, tell us that things exist which can be counted or which can be measured. The whole claim, however elaborate, still requires its point of suspension. We may put their claims to absolute or necessary truth as high as we please; but they cannot give us by themselves a single fact. I can show, for example, that a circle has an infinite number of properties, all of which are virtually implied in the very existence of a circle. But that the circle or that space itself exists, is not a necessary truth, but a datum of experience. It is quite true that such truths are not, in one sense, empirical; they can be discovered without any change of experience; for, by their very nature, they refer to the constant element of experience, and are true on the supposition of the absolute change- lessness of the objects contemplated. But it is a fallacy to suppose that, because independent of particular experiences, they are, therefore, indepen- dent of experience in general.

Now, if we agree, as Huxley would have agreed, that Hume's doctrine is true, if we cannot know a single fact except from experience, we are limited in moral questions, as in all others, to elaborating and analysing our experience, and can never properly transcend it. A scientific treatment of an ethical question, at any rate, must take for granted all the facts of human nature. It can show what morality actually is; what are, in fact, the motives which make men moral, and what are the consequences of moral conduct. But it cannot get outside of the universe and lay down moral principles independent of all influences. I am well aware that in speaking of ethical questions upon this ground, I am exposed to many expressions of metaphysical contempt. I may hope to throw light upon the usual working of morality; but my theory of the facts cannot make men moral of itself. I cannot hope, for example, to show that immorality involves a contradiction, for I know that immorality exists. I cannot even hope to show that it is necessarily productive of misery to the individual, for I know that some people take pleasure in vicious conduct. I cannot deduce facts from morals, for I must consistently regard morals as part of the observed consequences of human nature under given conditions. Metaphysicians may, if they can, show me a more excellent method. I admit that their language sometimes enables them to take what, in words at least, is a sublimer position than mine. Kant's famous phrase, "Thou must, therefore thou canst," is impressive. And yet, it seems to me to involve an obvious piece of logical juggling. It is quite true that whenever it is my duty to act in a certain way, it must be a possibility; but that is only because an impossibility cannot be a duty. It is not my duty to fly, because I have not wings; and conversely, no doubt, it would follow that *if* it were my duty I must possess the organs required. Thus understood, however, the phrase loses its sublimity, and yet, it is only because we have so to understand it, that it has any plausibility. Admitting, however, that people who differ from me

can use grander language, and confessing my readi-
ness to admit error whenever they can point to a
single fact attainable by the pure reason, I must
keep to the humbler path. I speak of the moral instincts as of others, simply from the point of view of
experience: I cannot myself discover a single truth
from the abstract principle of non-contradiction; and
am content to take for granted that the world exists
as we know it to exist, without seeking to deduce its
peculiarities by any high *à priori* road.

Upon this assumption, the question really resolves
itself into a different one. We can neither explain nor
justify the existence of pain; but, of course, we can
ask whether, as a matter of fact, pain predominates
over pleasure; and we can ask whether, as a matter
of fact, the "cosmic processes" tend to promote or
discourage virtuous conduct. Does the theory of the
"struggle for existence" throw any new light upon
the general problem? I am quite unable to see, for
my own part, that it really makes any difference:
evil exists; and the question whether evil predominates over good, can only, I should say, be
decided by an appeal to experience. One source of
evil is the conflict of interests. Every beast preys
upon others; and man, according to the old saying, is
a wolf to man. All that the Darwinian or any other
theory can do is, to enable us to trace the con-

sequences of this fact in certain directions; but it neither creates the fact nor makes it more or less an essential part of the process. It "explains" certain phenomena, in the sense of showing their connection with previous phenomena, but does not show why the phenomena should present themselves at all. If we indulge our minds in purely fanciful constructions, we may regard the actual system as good or bad, just as we choose to imagine for its alternative a better or a worse system. If everybody had been put into a world where there was no pain, or where each man could get all he wanted without interfering with his neighbours, we may fancy that things would have been pleasanter. If the struggle, which we all know to exist, had no effect in preventing the "survival of the fittest," things—so, at least, some of us may think—would have been worse. But such fancies have nothing to do with scientific inquiries. We have to take things as they are and make the best of them.

The common feeling, no doubt, is different. The incessant struggle between different races suggests a painful view of the universe, as Hobbes' natural state of war suggested painful theories as to human nature. War is evidently immoral, we think; and a doctrine which makes the whole process of evolution a process of war must be radically immoral too. The struggle, it is said, demands "ruthless self-assertion" and the hunting down of all competitors; and such phrases certainly have an unpleasant sound. But in the first place, the use of the epithets implies an anthropomorphism to which we have no right so long as we are dealing with the inferior species. We are then in a region to which such ideas have no direct application, and where the moral sentiments exist only in germ, if they can properly be said to exist at all. Is it fair to call a wolf ruthless because he eats a sheep and fails to consider the transaction from the sheep's point of view? We must surely admit that if the wolf is without mercy he is also without malice. We call an animal ferocious because a man who acted in the same way would be ferocious. But the man is really ferocious because he is really aware of the pain which he inflicts. The wolf, I suppose, has no more recognition of the sheep's feelings than a man has of feelings in the oyster or the potato. For him, they are simply non-existent; and it is just as inappropriate to think of the wolf as cruel, as it would be to call the sheep cruel for eating grass. Are we to say that "nature" is cruel because the arrangement increases the sum of undeserved suffering? That is a problem which I do not feel able to examine; but it is, at least, obvious that it cannot be answered off-hand in the affirmative. To the individual sheep it matters nothing whether he is eaten by the wolf or dies of disease or starvation. He has to die any way, and the particular way is unimportant. The wolf is simply one of the limiting forces upon sheep, and if he were removed others would come into play. The sheep, left to himself, would still give a practical illustration of the doctrine of Malthus. If, as evolutionists tell us, the hostility of the wolf tends to improve the breed of sheep, to encourage him to think more and to sharpen his wits, the sheep may be, on the whole, the better for the wolf, in this sense at least : that the sheep of a wolfless region might lead a more wretched existence, and be less capable animals and more subject to disease and starvation than the sheep in a wolf-haunted region. The wolf may, so far, be a blessing in disguise.

This suggests another obvious remark. When we speak of the struggle for existence, the popular view seems to construe this into the theory that the world is a mere cockpit, in which one race carries on an interminable struggle with the other. If the wolves are turned in with the sheep, the first result will be that all the sheep will become mutton, and the last that there will be one big wolf with all the others inside him. But this is contrary to the essence of the doctrine. Every race depends, we all hold, upon its environment, and the environment includes all the other races. If some, therefore, are in conflict, others are mutually necessary. If the wolf ate all the sheep, and the sheep ate all the grass, the result would be the extirpation of all the sheep and all the wolves, as well as all the grass. The struggle necessarily implies reciprocal dependence in a countless variety of ways. There is not only a conflict, but a system of tacit alliances. One species is necessary to the existence of others, though the multiplication of some implies also the dying out of particular rivals. The conflict implies no cruelty, as I have said, and the alliance no goodwill. The wolf neither loves the sheep (except as mutton) nor hates him; but he depends upon him as absolutely as if he were aware of the fact. The sheep is one of the wolf's necessaries of life. When we speak of the struggle for existence we mean, of course, that there is at any given period a certain equilibrium between all the existing species; it changes, though it changes so slowly that the process is imperceptible and difficult to realise even to the scientific imagination. The survival of any species involves the disappearance of rivals no more than the preservation of allies. The struggle, therefore, is so far from internecine that it necessarily involves co-operation. It cannot even be said that it necessarily implies suffering. People, indeed, speak as though the extinction of a race involved suffering in the same way as the slaughter of an individual. It is plain that this is not a necessary, though it may sometimes be the actual result. A corporation may be suppressed without injury to its members. Every individual will die before long, struggle or no struggle. If the rate of reproduction fails to keep up with the rate of extinction, the species must diminish. But this might happen without any increase of suffering. If the boys in a district discovered how to take birds' eggs, they might soon extirpate a species; but it does not follow that the birds would individually suffer. Perhaps they would feel themselves relieved from a disagreeable responsibility. The process by which a species is improved, the dying out of the least fit, implies no more suffering than we know to exist independently of any doctrine as to a struggle. When we use anthropomorphic language, we may speak of "self-assertion". But "self-assertion," minus the anthropomorphism, means self-preservation; and that is merely a way of describing the fact that an animal or plant which is well adapted to its conditions of life is more likely to live than an animal which is ill-adapted. I have some difficulty in imagining how any other arrangement can even be supposed possible. It seems to be almost an identical proposition that the healthiest and strongest will generally live longest ; and the conception of a " struggle for exist-ence " only enables us to understand how this results in certain progressive modifications of the species. If we could ever for a moment have fancied that there was no pain and disease, and that some beings were not more liable than others to those evils, I might admit that the new doctrine has made the world darker. As it is, it seems to me that it leaves the data just what they were before, and only shows us that they have certain previously unsuspected bearings upon the history of the world.

One other point must be mentioned. Not only are species interdependent as well as partly in com-petition, but there is an absolute dependence in all the higher species between its different members which may be said to imply a *de facto* altruism, as the dependence upon other species implies a *de facto* co-operation. Every animal, to say nothing else, is absolutely dependent for a considerable part of its existence upon its parents. The young bird or beast could not grow up unless its mother took care of it for a certain period. There is, therefore, no struggle as between mother and progeny ; but, on the con-trary, the closest possible alliance. Otherwise, life would be impossible. The young being defenceless, their parents could exterminate them if they pleased, and by so doing would exterminate the race. The parental relation, of course, constantly involves a partial sacrifice of the mother to her young. She has to go through a whole series of operations, which strain her own strength and endanger her own existence, but which are absolutely essential to the continuance of the race. It may be anthropomorphic to attribute any maternal emotions of the human kind to the animal. The bird, perhaps, sits upon her eggs because they give her an agreeable sensation, or, if you please, from a blind instinct which somehow determines her to the practice. She does not look forward, we may suppose, to bringing up a family, or speculate upon the delights of domestic affection. I only say that as a fact she behaves in a way which is at once injurious to her own chances of individual survival, and absolutely necessary to the survival of the species. The abnormal bird who deserts her nest escapes many dangers; but if all birds were devoid of the instinct, the birds would not survive a generation.

Now, I ask, what is the difference which takes place when the monkey gradually loses his tail and sets up a superior brain? Is it properly to be described as a development or improvement of the "cosmic process," or as the beginning of a prolonged contest against it?

In the first place, so far as man becomes a reasonable being, capable of foresight and of the adoption of means to ends, he recognises the nature of these tacit alliances. He believes it to be his interest not to exterminate everything, but to exterminate those species alone whose existence is incompatible with his own. The wolf eats every sheep that he comes across as long as his appetite lasts. If there are too many wolves, the process is checked by the starvation of the supernumerary eaters. Man can maintain just as many sheep as he wants, and may also proportion the numbers of his own species to the possibilities of future supply. Many of the lower species thus become subordinate parts of the social organism— that is to say, of the new equilibrium which has been established. There is so far a reciprocal advantage. The sheep that is preserved with a view to mutton gets the advantage, though he is not kept with a view to his own advantage. Of all arguments for vegetarianism, none is so weak as the argument from humanity. The pig has a stronger interest than any one in the demand for bacon. If all the world were Jewish, there would be no pigs at all. He has to pay for his privileges by an early death; but he makes a good bargain of it. He dies young, and, though we can hardly infer the "love of the gods," we must admit that he gets a superior race of beings to attend to his comforts, moved by the strongest possible interest in his health and vigour, and induced by its own needs, perhaps, to make him a little too fat for comfort, but certainly also to see that he has a good sty, and plenty to eat every day of his life. Other races, again, are extirpated as "ruthlessly" as in the merely instinctive struggle for existence. We get rid of wolves and snakes as well as we can, and more systematically than can be done by their animal competitors. The process does not necessarily involve cruelty, and certainly does not involve a diminution of the total of happiness. The struggle for existence means the substitution of a new system of equilibrium, in which one of the old discords has been removed, and the survivors live in greater harmony. If the wolf is extirpated as an internecine enemy, it is that there may be more sheep when sheep have become our allies and the objects of our earthly providence. The result may be, perhaps I might say must be, a state in which, on the whole, there is a greater amount of life supported on the planet; and therefore, as those will think who are not pessimists, a decided gain on the balance. At any rate, the difference so far is that the condition which was in all cases necessary, is now consciously recognised as necessary; and that we deliberately aim at a result which always had to be achieved on

penalty of destruction. So far, again, as morality
can be established on purely prudential grounds, the
same holds good of relations between human beings
themselves. Men begin to perceive that, even from
a purely personal point of view, peace is preferable
to war. If war is unhappily still prevalent, it is at
least not war in which every clan is fighting with its
neighbours, and where conquest means slavery or
extirpation. Millions of men are at peace within the
limits of a modern State, and can go about their
business without cutting each other's throats. When
they fight with other nations they do not enslave nor
massacre their prisoners. Starting from the purely
selfish ground Hobbes could prove conclusively that
everybody benefited by the social compact which substituted peace and order for the original state of war.
Is this, then, a reversal of the old state of things—a
combating of a "cosmic process"? I should rather
say that it is a development of the tacit alliances,
and a modification so far of the direct or internecine
conflict. Both were equally implied in the older
conditions, and both still exist. Some races form
alliances, while others are crowded out of existence.
Of course, I cease to do some things which I should
have done before. I don't attack the first man I
meet in the street and take his scalp. One reason is
that I don't expect he will take mine ; for, if I did, I

fear that, even as a civilised being, I should try to anticipate his intentions. This merely means that we have both come to see that we have a common interest in keeping the peace. And this, again, merely means that the tacit alliance which was always an absolutely necessary condition of the survival of the species has now been extended through a wider area. The species could not have got on at all if there had not been so much alliance as is necessary for its reproduction and for the preservation of its young for some years of helplessness. The change is simply that the small circle which included only the primitive family or class has extended, so that we can meet members of the same nation, or, it may be, of the same race, on terms which were previously confined to the minor group. We have still to exterminate and still to preserve. The mode of employing our energies has changed, but not the essential nature. Morality proper, however, has so far not emerged. It begins when sympathy begins; when we really desire the happiness of others; or, as Kant says, when we treat other men as an end and not simply as a means. Undoubtedly this involves a new principle, no less than the essential principle of all true morality. Still, I have to ask whether it implies a combating or a continuation of a cosmic process. Now, as I have observed, even the animal mother shows what I have called a *de facto* altruism. She has instincts which, though dangerous to the individual, are essential for the race. The human mother sacrifices herself with a consciousness of the results to herself, and her personal fears are overcome by the strength of her affections. She intentionally endures a painful death to save them from suffering. The animal sacrifices herself, but without foresight of the result, and therefore without moral worth. This is merely the most striking exemplification of the general process of the development of morality. Conduct is first regarded purely with a view to the effects upon the agent, and is therefore enforced by extrinsic penalties, by consequences, that is, supposed to be attached to us by the will of some ruler, natural or supernatural. The instinct which comes to regard such conduct as bad in itself, which implies a dislike of giving pain to others, and not merely a dislike to the gallows, grows up under such probation until the really moralised being acquires feelings which make the external penalty superfluous. This, indubitably, is the greatest of all changes, the critical fact which decides whether we are to regard conduct simply as useful, or also to regard it as moral in the strictest sense. But I should still call it a development and not a reversal of the previous process. The conduct

which we call virtuous is the same conduct externally
which we before regarded as useful. The difference
is that the simple fact of its utility, that is, of its
utility to others and to the race in general, has now
become also the sufficient motive for the action as
well as the implicit cause of the action. In the
earlier stages, when no true sympathy existed, men
and animals were still forced to act in a certain way
because it was beneficial to others. They now act
in that way because they are conscious that it is
beneficial to others. The whole history of moral
evolution seems to imply this. We may go back to a
period at which the moral law is identified with the
general customs of the race ; at which there is no
perception of any clear distinction between that
which is moral and that which is simply customary ;
between that which is imposed by a law in the strict
sense and that which is dictated by general moral
principles. In such a state of things, the motives for
obedience partake of the nature of " blind instincts ".
No definite reason for them is present to the mind of
the agent, and it does not occur to him even to demand a reason. " Our fathers did so and we do so "
is the sole and sufficient explanation of their conduct.
Thus instinct again may be traced back by evolutionists to the earliest period at which the instincts
implied in the relations between the sexes or between

parents and offspring, existed. They were the germ from which has sprung all morality such as we now recognise.

Morality, then, implies the development of certain instincts which are essential to the race, but which may, in an indefinite number of cases, be injurious to the individual. The particular mother is killed because she obeys her natural instincts; but, if it were not for mothers and their instincts, the race would come to an end. Professor Huxley speaks of the "fanatical individualism" of our time as failing to construct morality from the analogy of the cosmic process. An individualism which regards the cosmic process as equivalent simply to an internecine struggle of each against all, must certainly fail to construct a satisfactory morality upon such terms, and I will add that any individualism which fails to recognise fully the social character, which regards society as an aggregate instead of an organism, will, in my opinion, find itself in difficulties. But I also submit that the development of the instincts which directly correspond to the needs of the race, is merely another case in which we aim consciously at an end which was before an unintentional result of our actions. Every race, above the lowest, has instincts which are only intelligible by the requirements of the race; and has both to compete with some and to form alliances with others of its fellow occupants of the planet. Both in the unmoralised condition and in that in which morality has become most developed, these instincts have common characteristics, and may be regarded as conditions of the power of the race to which they belong to maintain its position in the world, and, speaking roughly, to preserve or increase its own vitality.

I will not pause to insist upon this so far as regards many qualities which are certainly moral, though they may be said to refer primarily to the individual. That chastity and temperance, truthfulness and energy, are, on the whole, advantages both to the individual and to the race, does not, I fancy, require elaborate proof; nor need I argue at length that the races in which they are common will therefore have inevitable advantages in the struggle for existence. Of all qualities which enable a race to hold its own, none is more important than the power of organising individually, politically, and socially, and that power implies the existence of justice and the instinct of mutual confidence—in short, all the social virtues. The difficulty seems to be felt in regard to those purely altruistic impulses, which, at first glance at any rate, make it apparently our duty to preserve those who would otherwise be unfit to live. Virtue, says Professor Huxley, is directed "not so much to the survival of the fittest," as to the "fitting of as many as possible to survive". I do not dispute the statement, I think it true in a sense; but I have a difficulty as to its application.

Morality, it is obvious, must be limited by the conditions in which we are placed. What is impossible is not a duty. One condition plainly is that the planet is limited. There is only room for a certain number of living beings; and though we may determine what shall be the number, we cannot arbitrarily say that it shall be indefinitely great. It is one consequence that we do, in fact, go on suppressing the unfit, and cannot help going on suppressing them. Is it desirable that it should be otherwise? Should we wish, for example, that America could still be a hunting-ground for savages? Is it better that it should contain a million red men or sixty millions of civilised whites? Undoubtedly the moralist will say with absolute truth that the methods of extirpation adopted by Spaniards and Englishmen were detestable. I need not say that I agree with him, and hope that such methods may be abolished wherever any remnant of them exists. But I say so partly because I believe in the struggle for existence. This process underlies morality, and operates whether we are moral or not. The most civilised race, that which has the greatest knowledge, skill, power of

organisation, will, I hold, have an inevitable advantage in the struggle, even if it does not use the brutal
means which are superfluous as well as cruel. All
the natives who lived in America a hundred years
ago would be dead now in any case, even if they had
invariably been treated with the greatest humanity,
fairness, and consideration. Had they been unable
to suit themselves to new conditions of life, they
would have suffered an euthanasia instead of a partial
extirpation; and had they suited themselves they
would either have been absorbed or become a useful
part of the population. To abolish the old brutal
method is not to abolish the struggle for existence,
but to make the result depend upon a higher order of
qualities than those of the mere piratical viking.

Mr. Pearson has been telling us in his most interesting book, that the negro may not improbably
hold his own in Africa. I cannot say I regard this
as an unmixed evil. Why should there not be parts
of the world in which races of inferior intelligence or
energy should hold their own? I am not so anxious
to see the whole earth covered by an indefinite multiplication of the cockney type. But I only quote the
suggestion for another reason. Till recent years the
struggle for existence was carried on as between
Europeans and negroes by simple violence and
brutality. The slave trade and its consequences

have condemned the whole continent to barbarism. That, undoubtedly, was part of the struggle for existence. But, if Mr. Pearson's guess should be verified, the results have been so far futile as well as disastrous. The negro has been degraded, and yet, after all our brutality, we cannot take his place. Therefore, besides the enormous evils to slave-trading countries themselves, the lowering of their moral tone, the substitution of piracy for legitimate commerce, and the degradation of the countries which bought the slaves, the superior race has not even been able to suppress the inferior. But the abolition of this monstrous evil does not involve the abolition but the humanisation of the struggle. The white man, however merciful he becomes, may gradually extend over such parts of the country as are suitable to him; and the black man will hold the rest and acquire such arts and civilisation as he is capable of appropriating. The absence of cruelty would not alter the fact that the fittest race would extend; but it may ensure that whatever is good in the negro may have a chance of development in his own sphere, and that success in the struggle will be decided by more valuable qualities.

Without venturing further into a rather speculative region, I need only indicate the bearing of such considerations upon problems nearer home. It is often complained that the tendency of modern civilisation is to preserve the weakly, and therefore to lower the vitality of the race. This seems to involve inadmissible assumptions. In the first place, the process by which the weaker are preserved consists in suppressing various conditions unfavourable to human life in general. Sanitary legislation, for example, aims at destroying the causes of many of the diseases from which our forefathers suffered. If we can suppress the smallpox, we of course save many weakly children, who would have died had they been attacked. But we also remove one of the causes which weakened the constitutions of many of the survivors. I do not know by what right we can say that such legislation, or again, the legislation which prevents the excessive labour of children, does more harm by preserving the weak than it does good by preventing the weakening of the strong. One thing is at any rate clear: to preserve life is to increase the population, and therefore to increase the competition; or, in other words, to intensify the struggle for existence. The process is as broad as it is long. If we could be sure that every child born should grow up to maturity, the result would be to double the severity of the competition for support. What we should have to show, therefore, in order to justify the inference of a deterioration due to this process, would be, not that it simply increased the number of the candidates for living, but that it gave to the feebler candidates a differential advantage; that they are now more fitted than they were before for ousting their superior neighbours from the chances of support. But I can see no reason for supposing such a consequence to be probable or even possible. The struggle for existence, as I have suggested, rests upon the unalterable facts that the world is limited and population elastic. Under all conceivable circumstances we shall still have in some way or other to proportion our numbers to our supplies; and under all circumstances those who are fittest by reason of intellectual or moral or physical qualities will have the best chance of occupying good places, and leaving descendants to supply the next generation. It is surely not less true that in the civilised as much as in the most barbarous race, the healthiest are the most likely to live, and the most likely to be ancestors. If so, the struggle will still be carried on upon the same principles, though certainly in a different shape.

It is true that this suggests one of the most difficult questions of the time. It is suggested, for example, that in some respects the "highest" specimens of the race are not the healthiest or the fittest. Genius, according to some people, is a variety of disease, and intellectual power is won by a diminution of reproductive power. A lower race, again, if we measure "high" and "low" by intellectual capacity, may oust a higher race, because it can support itself more cheaply, or, in other words, because it is more efficient for industrial purposes. Without presuming to pronounce upon such questions, I will simply ask whether this does not interpret Professor Huxley's remark about that "cosmic nature" which is still so strong, and which is likely to be strong so long as men require stomachs. We have not, I think, to suppress it, but to adapt it to new circumstances. We are engaged in working out a gigantic problem : What is the best, in the sense of the most efficient, type of human being? What is the best combination of brains and stomach? We turn out saints, who are "too good to live," and philosophers, who have run too rapidly to brains. They do not answer in practice, because they are instruments too delicate for the rough work of daily life. They may give us a foretaste of qualities which will be some day possible for the average man ; of intellectual and moral qualities, which, though now exceptional, may become commonplace. But the best stock for the race are those in whom we have been lucky enough to strike out the happy combination, in which greater intellectual power is produced without the loss of physical vigour. Such men, it is probable, will not deviate so widely from the average type. The reconciliation of the two conditions can only be effected by a very gradual process of slowly edging onwards in the right direction. Meanwhile the theory of a struggle for existence justifies us, instead of condemning us, for preserving the delicate child, who may turn out to be a Newton or a Keats, because he will leave to us the advantage of his discoveries or his poems, while his physical feebleness assures us that he will not propagate his race.

This may lead to a final question. Does the morality of a race strengthen or weaken it; fit it to hold its own in the general equilibrium, or make its extirpation by low moral races more probable? I do not suppose that anybody would deny what I have already suggested, that the more moral the race, the more harmonious and the better organised, the better it is fitted for holding its own. But if this be admitted, we must also admit that the change is not that it has ceased to struggle, but that it struggles by different means. It holds its own, not merely by brute force, but by justice, humanity, and intelligence, while, it may be added, the possession of such qualities does not weaken the brute force, where such a quality is still required. The most civilised races are, of course, also the most formidable in war. But, if we take the opposite alternative, I must ask how any quality which really weakens the vitality of the race can properly be called moral. I should entirely repudiate any rule of conduct which could be shown to have such a tendency. This, indeed, indicates what seems to me to be the moral difficulty with most people. Charity, you say, is a virtue; charity increases beggary, and so far tends to produce a feebler population; therefore, a moral quality tends doubly to diminish the vigour of a nation. The answer is, of course, obvious, and I am confident that Professor Huxley would have so far agreed with me. It is that all charity which fosters a degraded class is therefore immoral. The "fanatical individualism" of to-day has its weaknesses; but in this matter it seems to me that we see the weakness of the not less fanatical "collectivism".

The question, in fact, how far any of the socialistic or ethical schemes of to-day are right or wrong, depends upon our answer to the question how far they tend to produce a vigorous or an enervated population. If I am asked to subscribe to General Booth's scheme, I inquire first whether the scheme is likely to increase or diminish the number of helpless hangers-on upon the efficient part of society. Will the whole nation consist in larger proportions of active and responsible workers, or of people who are simply burdens upon the real workers? The answer decides not only the question whether it is expedient, but also the question whether it is right or wrong, to support the proposed scheme. Every charitable action is so far a good action that it implies sympathy for suffering; but if it is so much in want of prudence that it increases the evil which it means to remedy, it becomes for that reason a bad action. To develop sympathy without developing foresight is just one of the one-sided developments which fail to constitute a real advance in morality, though I will not deny that it may incidentally lead to an advance.

I hold, then, that the " struggle for existence " belongs to an underlying order of facts to which moral epithets cannot be properly applied. It denotes a condition of which the moralist has to take account, and to which morality has to be adapted; but which, just because it is a " cosmic process," cannot be altered, however much we may alter the conduct which it dictates. Under all conceivable circumstances, the race has to adapt itself to the environment, and that necessarily implies a conflict as well as an alliance. The preservation of the fittest, which is surely a good thing, is merely another aspect of the dying out of the unfit, which is hardly a bad thing. The feast which Nature spreads before us, according to Malthus's metaphor, is only sufficient for a limited number of guests, and the one question is how to select them. The tendency of morality is to humanise the struggle, to minimise the suffering of those who lose the game; and to offer the prizes to the qualities which are advantageous to all, rather than to those which increase and intensify the bitterness of the conflict. This implies the growth of foresight, which is an extension of the earlier instinct, and enables men to adapt themselves to the future and to learn from the past, as well as to act up to immediate impulse of present events. It implies still more the development of the sympathy which makes every man feel for the hurts of all, and which, as social organisation is closer, and the dependence of each constituent atom upon the whole organisation is more vividly realised, extends the range of a man's interests beyond his own private needs. In that sense, again, it must stimulate " collectivism " at the expense of a crude individualism, and condemns the doctrine which, as Professor Huxley puts it, would forbid us to restrain the member of a community from doing his best to destroy it. To restrain such conduct is surely to carry on the conflict against all anti-social agents or tendencies. For I should certainly hold any form of collectivism to be immoral which denied the essential doctrine of the abused individualist, the necessity, that is, for individual responsibility. We have surely to suppress the murderer, as our ancestors suppressed the wolf. We have to suppress both the external enemies, the noxious animals whose existence is incompatible with our own, and the internal enemies which are injurious elements in the society itself. That is, we have to work for the same end of eliminating the least fit. Our methods are changed; we desire to suppress poverty, not to extirpate the poor man. We give inferior races a chance of taking whatever place they are fit for, and try to supplant them with the least possible severity if they are unfit for any place. But the suppression of poverty supposes not the confiscation of wealth, which would hardly suppress poverty in the long run, nor even the adoption of a system of living which would enable the idle and the good-for-nothing to survive. The progress of civilisation depends, I should say, on the extension of the sense of duty which each man owes to society at large. That involves such a constitution of society that, although we abandon the old methods of hanging and flogging and shooting down—methods which corrupted the inflicters of punishment by diminishing their own sense of responsibility—may give an advantage to the prudent and industrious, and make it more probable that they will be the ancestors of the next generation. A system which should equalise the advantages of the energetic and the helpless would begin by demoralising, and would very soon lead to an unprecedented intensification of the struggle for existence. The probable result of a ruthless socialism would be the adoption of very severe means for suppressing those who did not contribute their share of work. But, in any case, as it seems, we never get away or break away from the inevitable fact. If individual ends could be suppressed, if every man worked for the good of society as energetically as for his own, we should still feel the absolute necessity of proportioning the whole body to the whole supplies obtainable from the planet, and to preserve the equilibrium of mankind relatively to the rest of nature. That day is probably distant; but even upon that hypothesis the struggle for existence would still be with us, and there would be the same necessity for preserving the fittest and killing out, as gently as might be, those who were unfit.

END OF VOL. I.